THIS DRAWING BOOK BELONGS TO

_____

_____

_____

How to draw step by step

We've created a sketch guide by following the steps
You must repeat and transfer and with the period
with the period you will find that you learn quickly

The first step is to draw the head in a simple way

The second step is to draw and the head of the abdomen and one of the wings

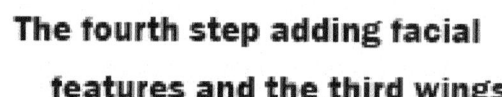

The third step is to draw the guilt and two wings

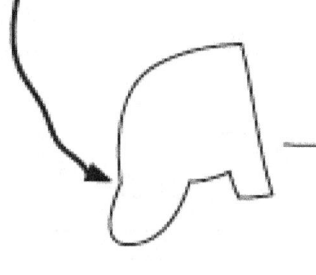

The fourth step adding facial features and the third wings

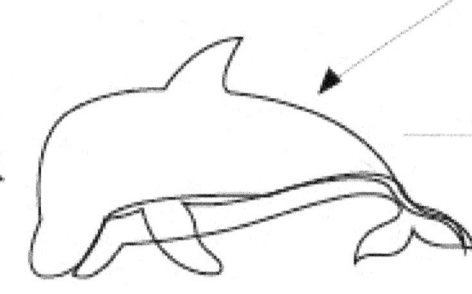

The fifth step adding some features of the face and abdomen

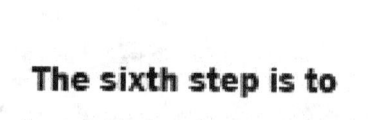

The sixth step is to add the final touches

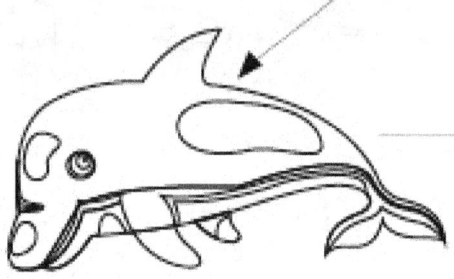

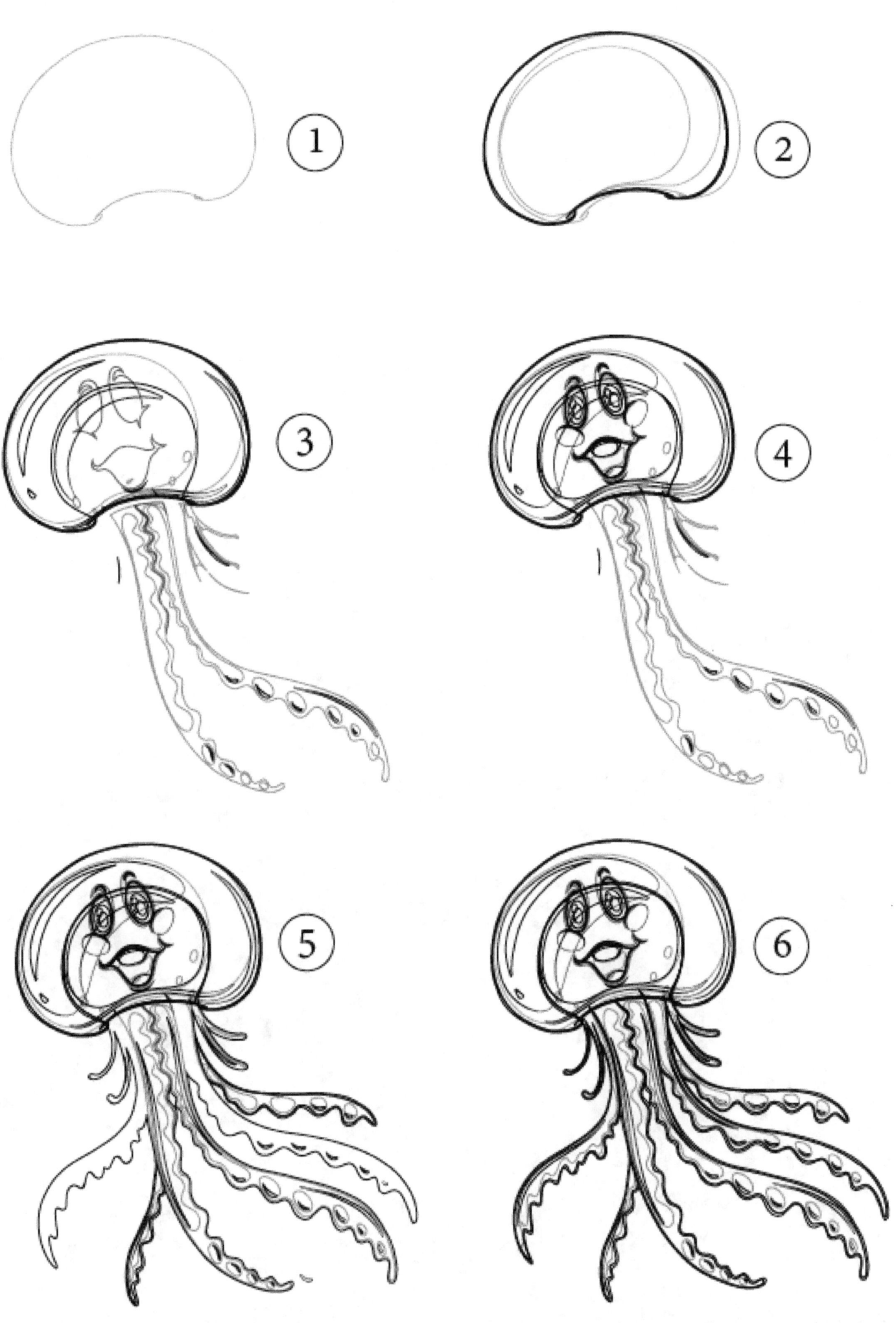

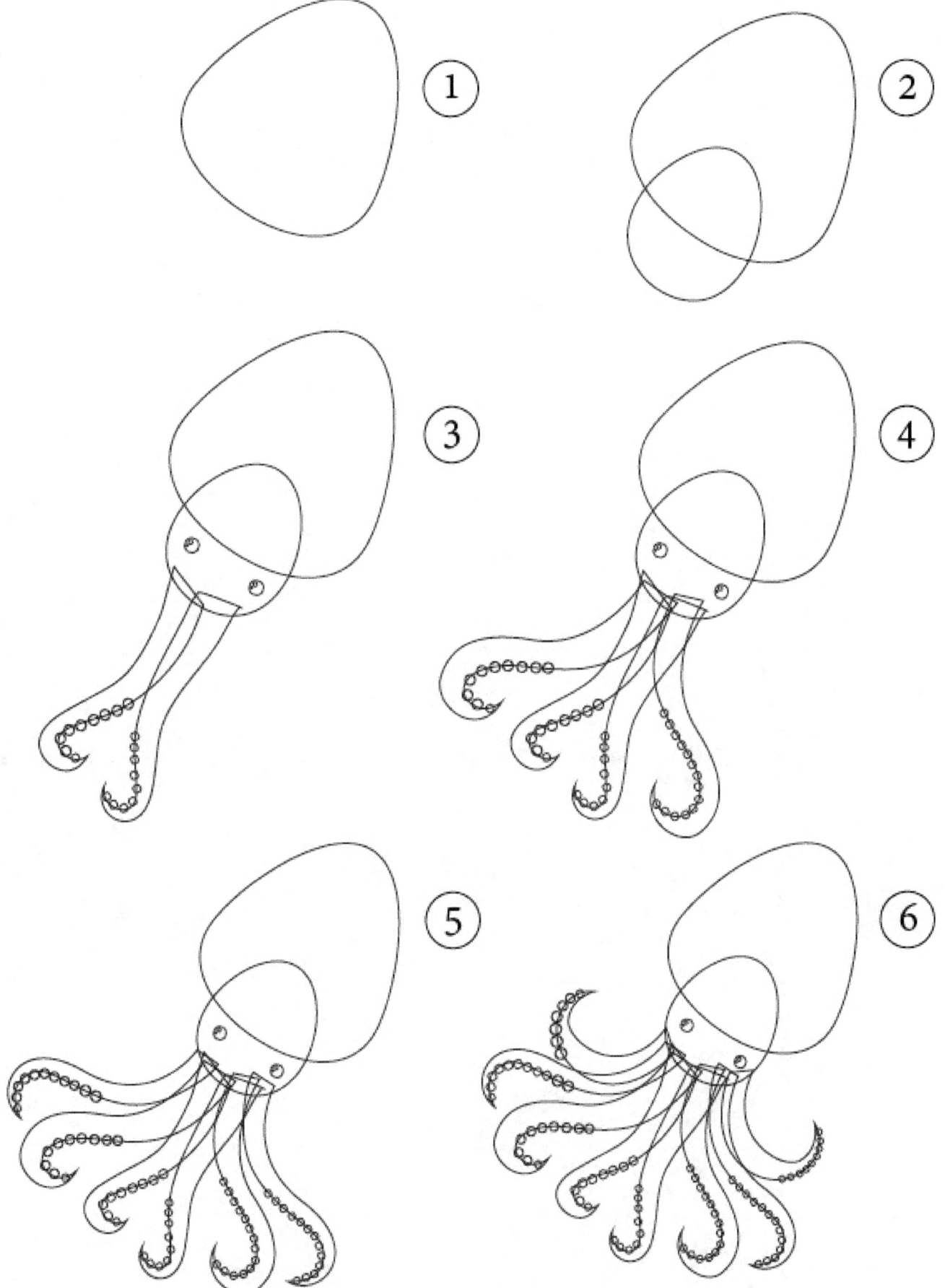

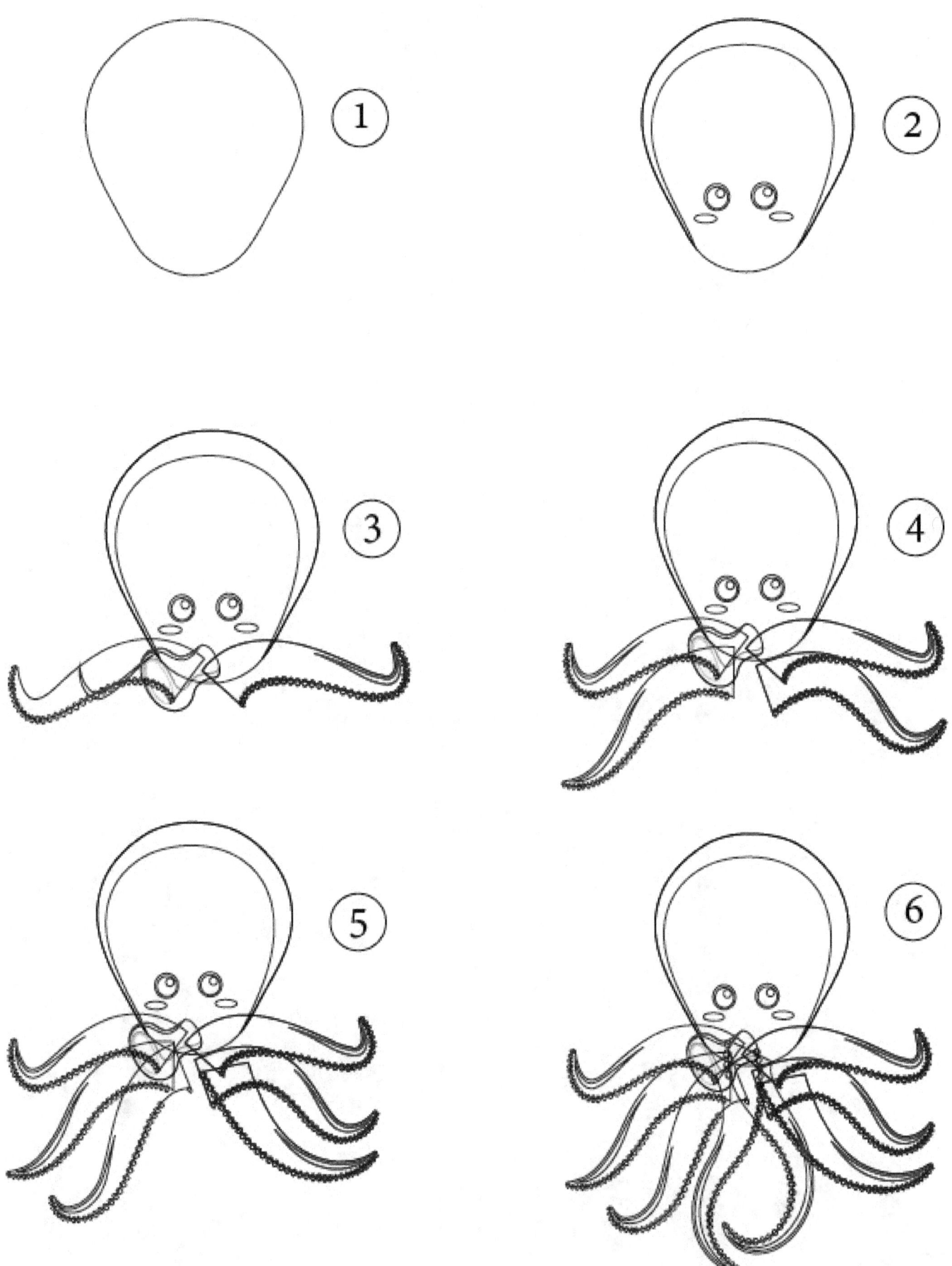

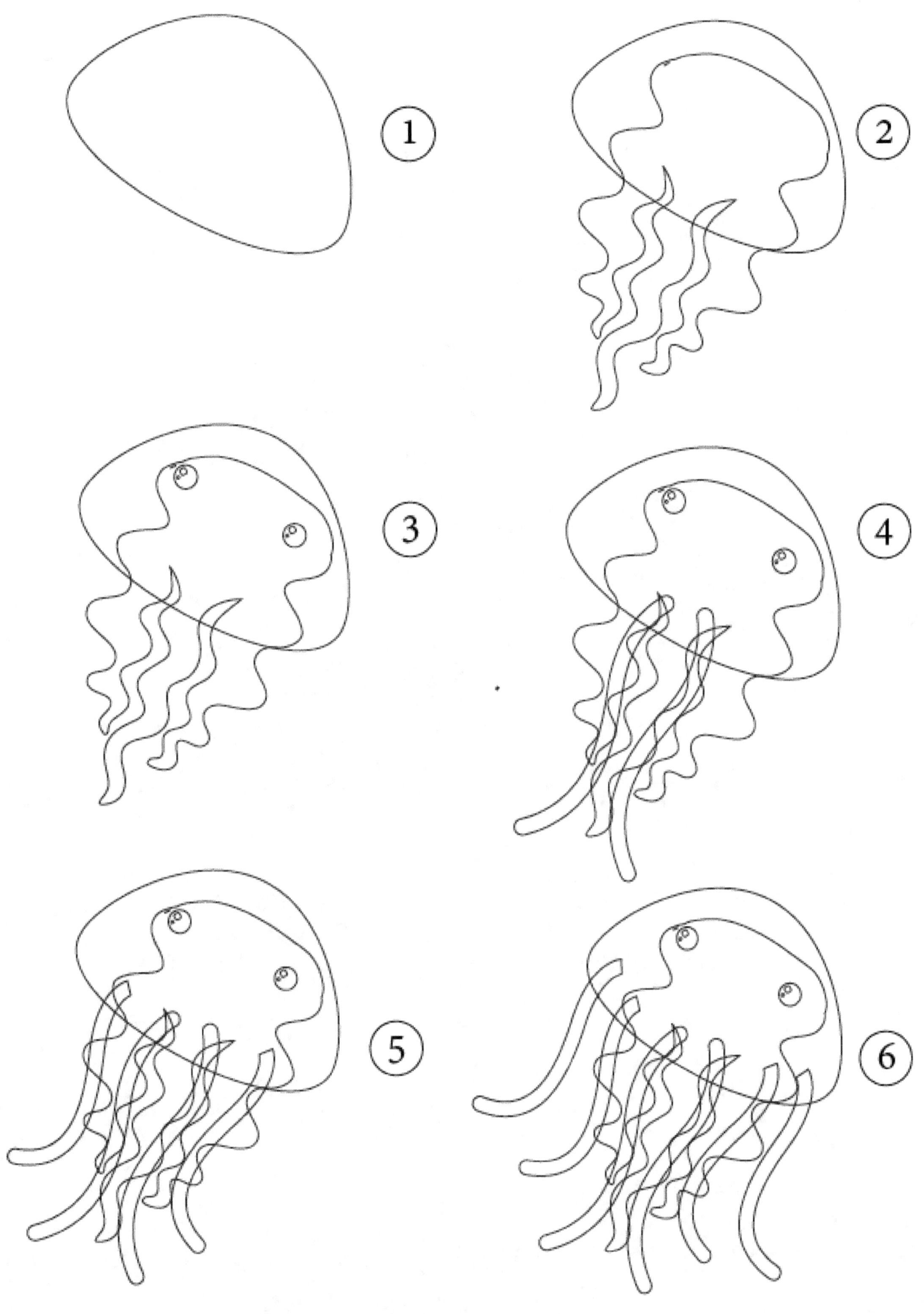

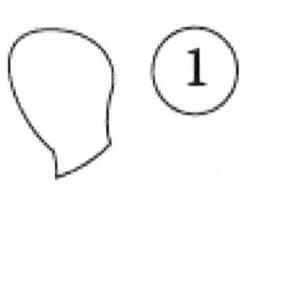
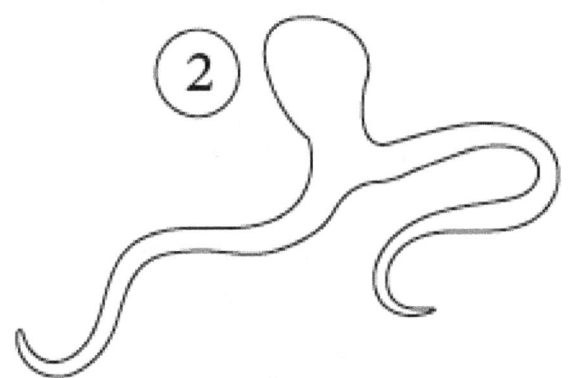
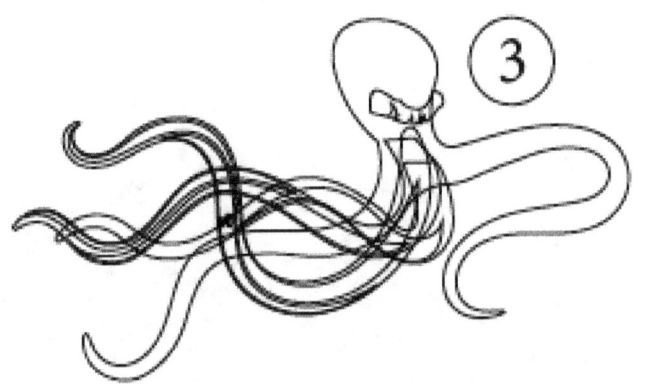
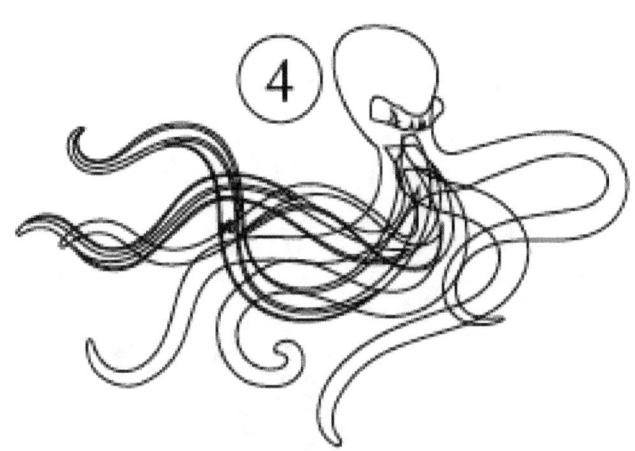
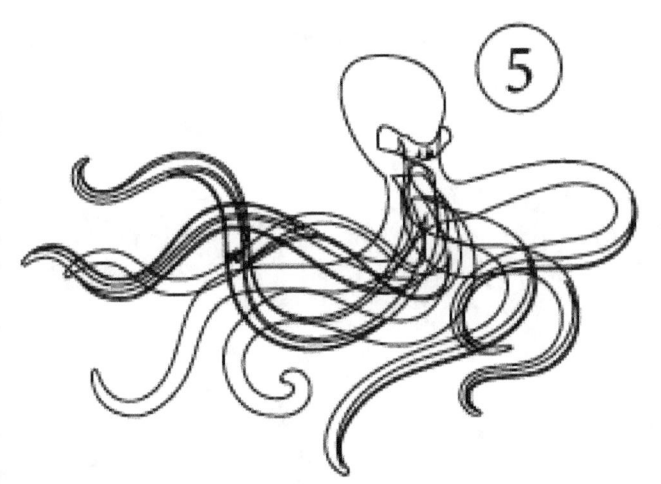

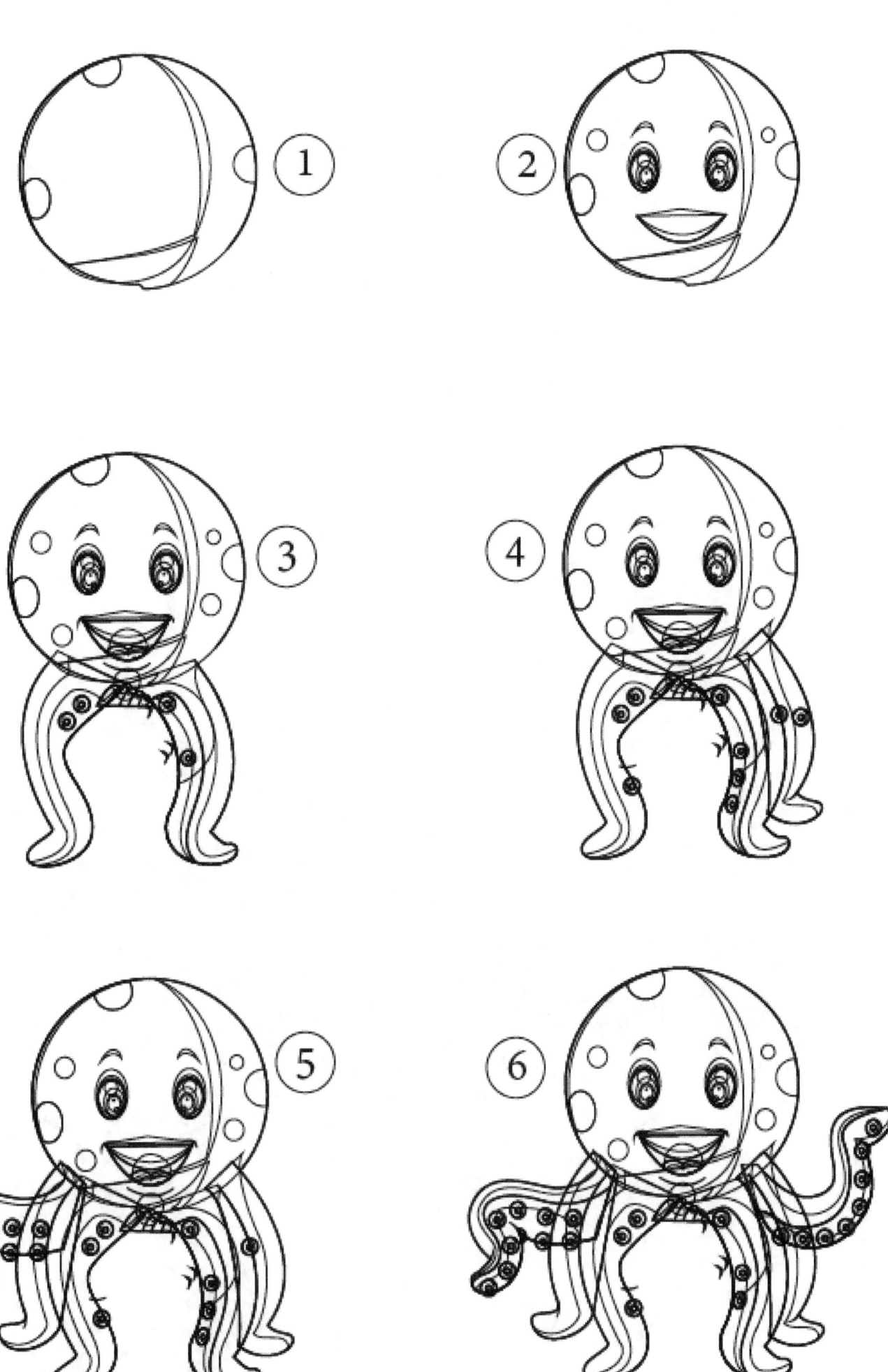

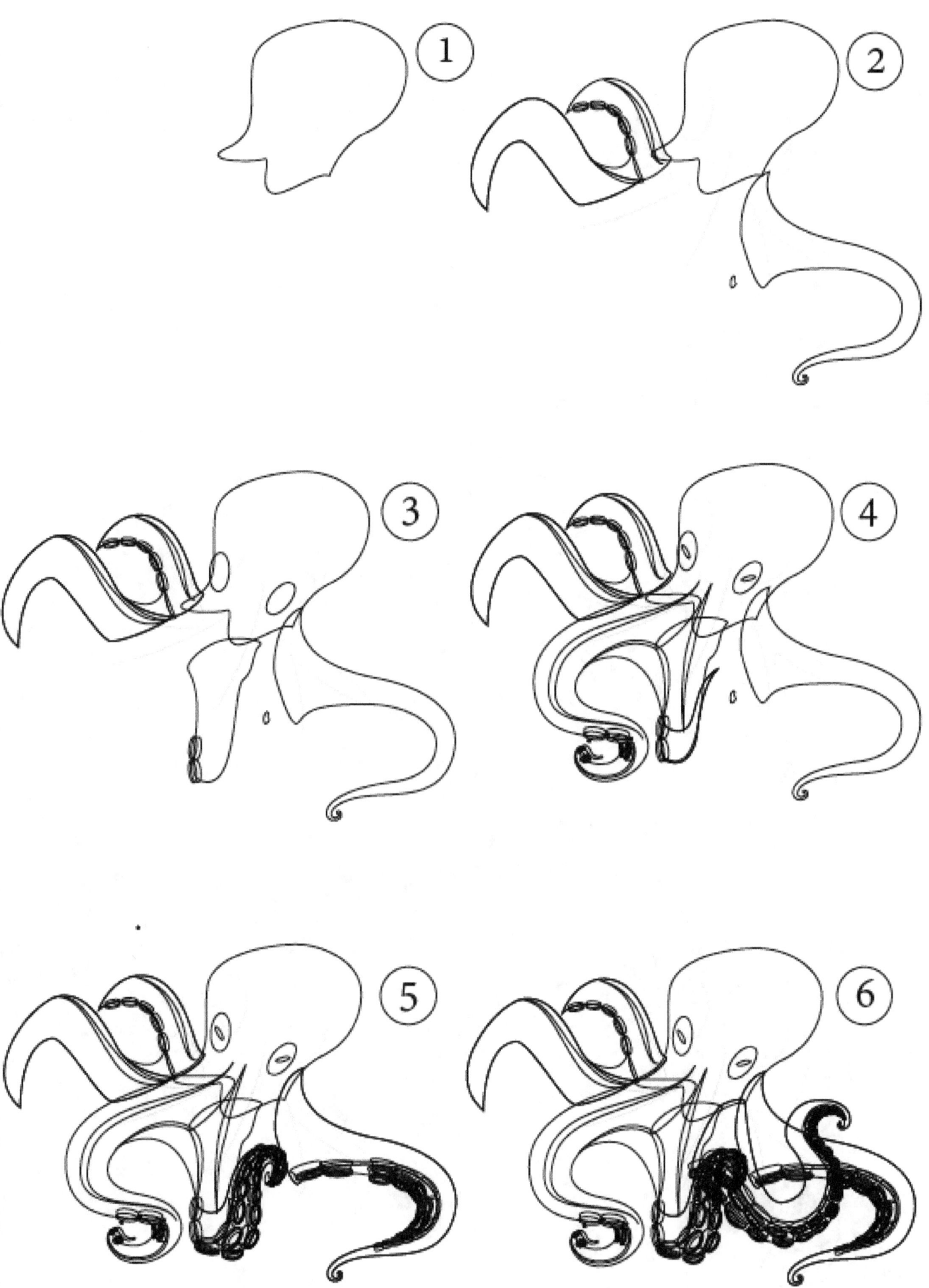

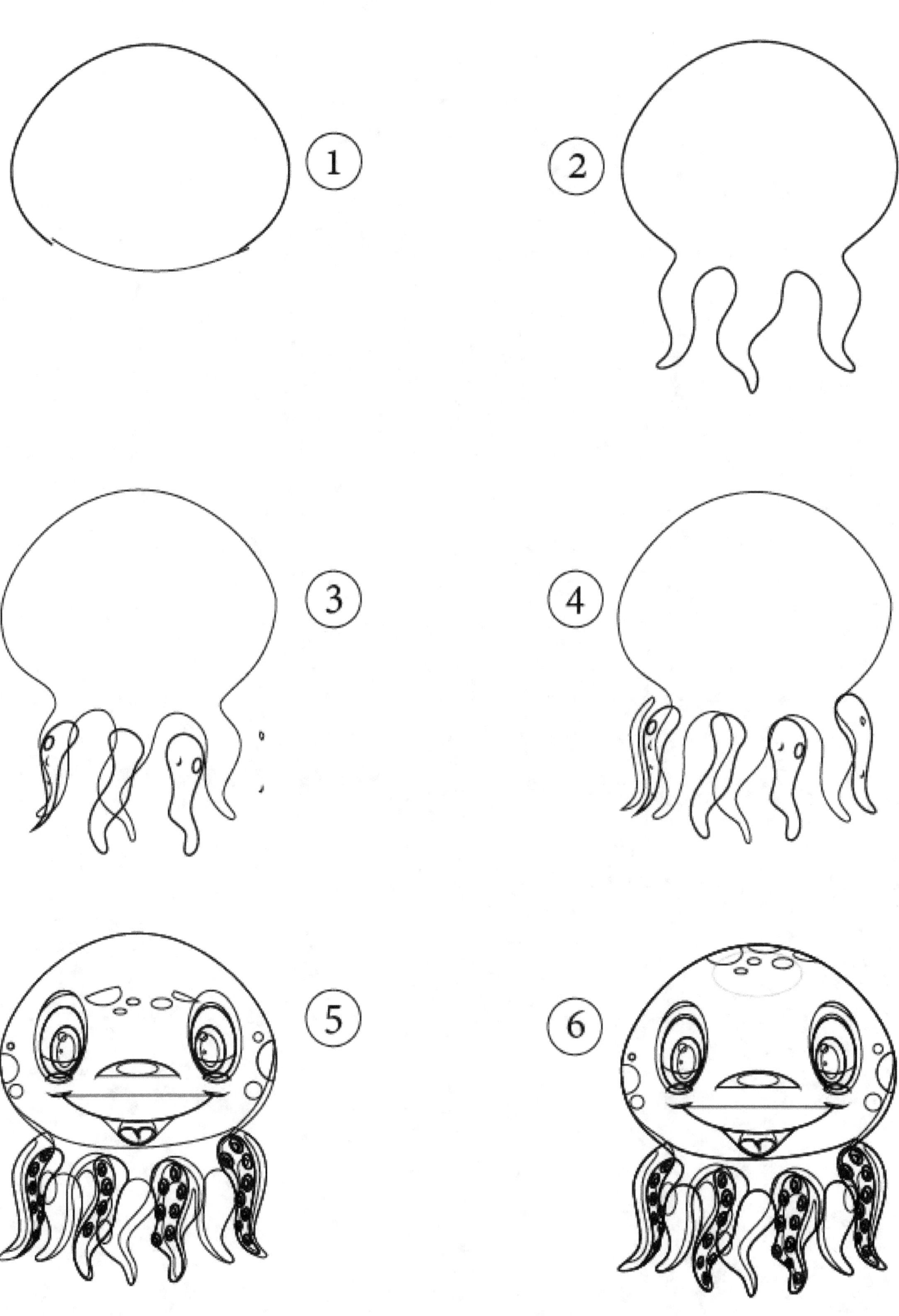

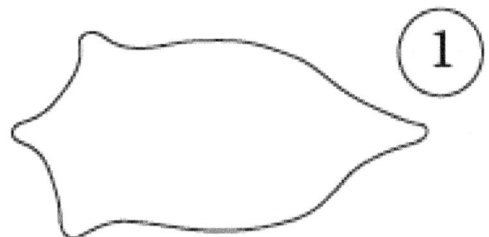
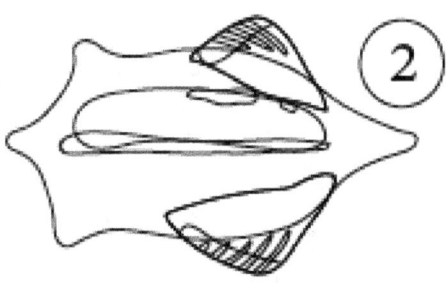
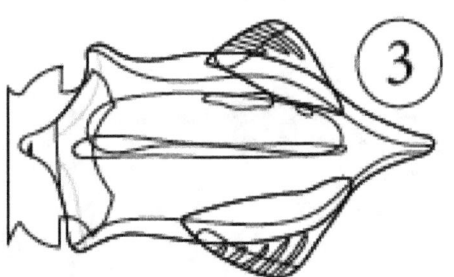
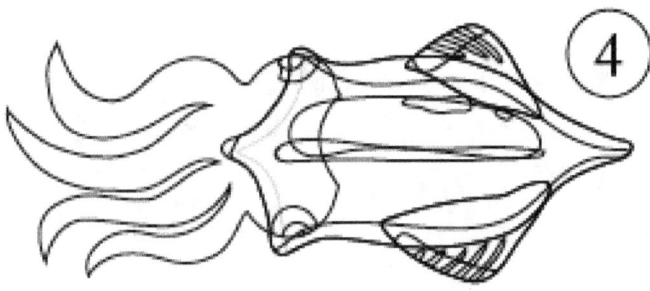

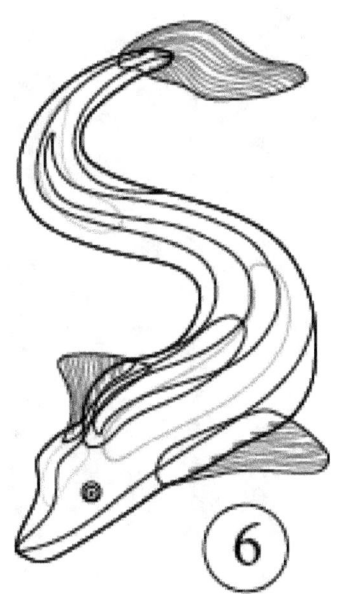

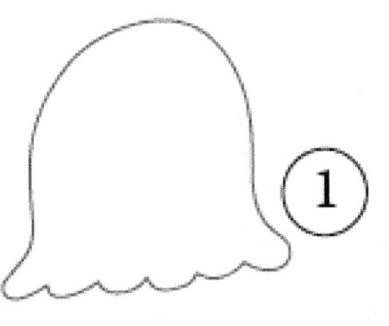
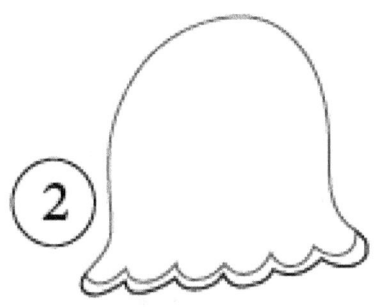
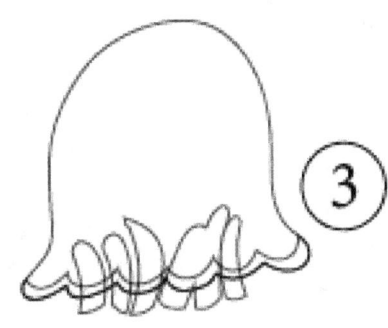
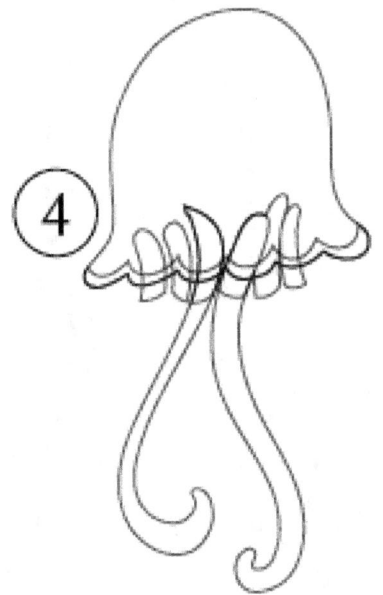
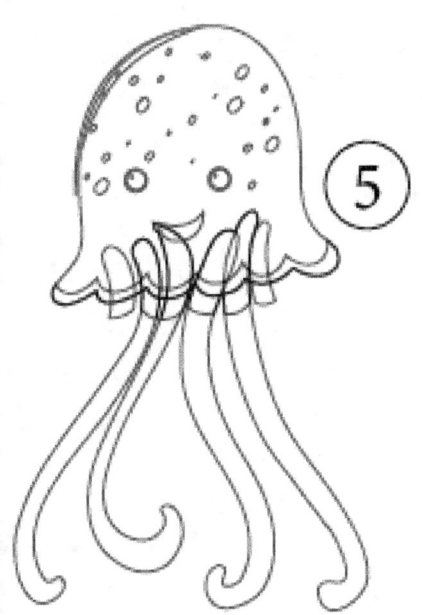
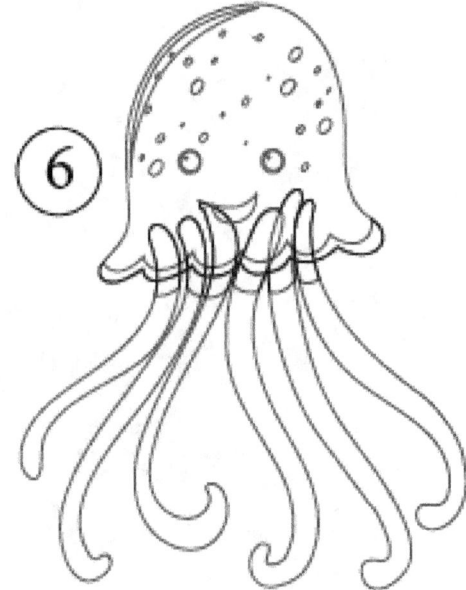

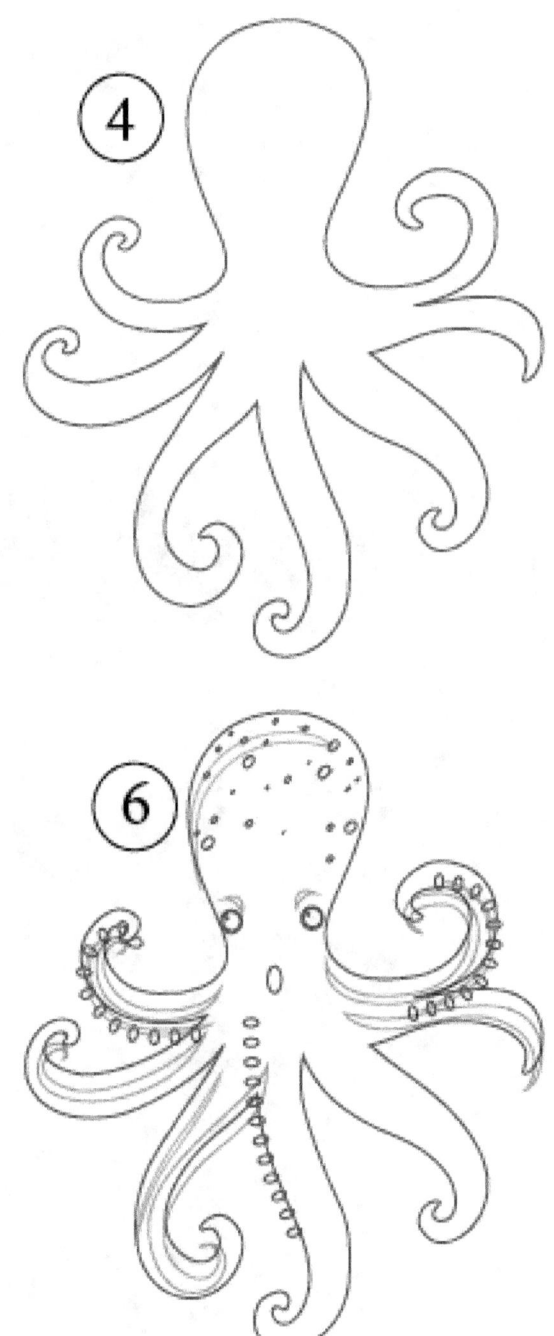

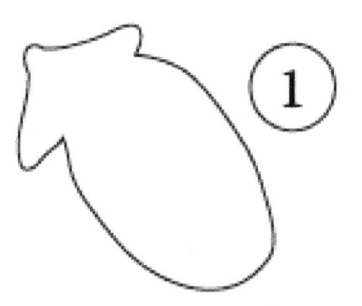
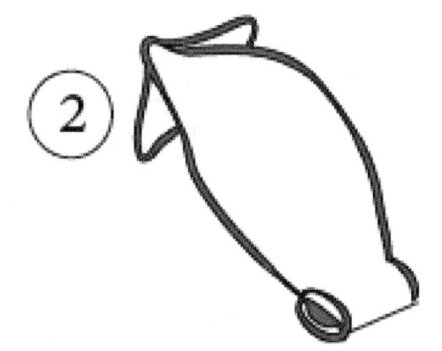

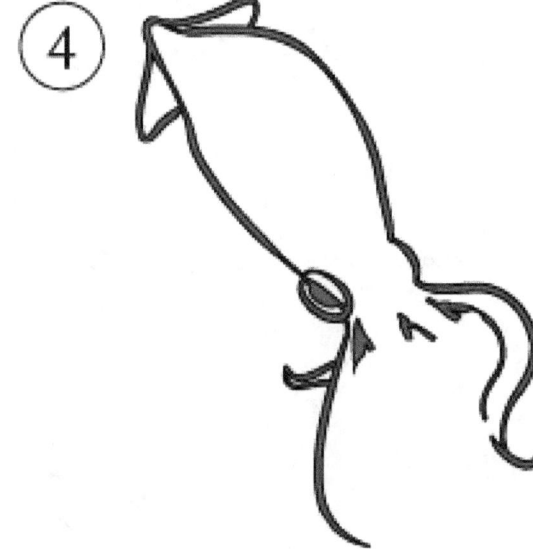

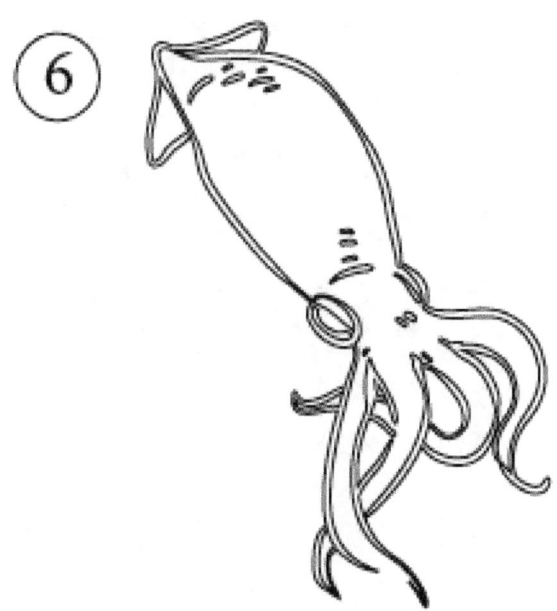

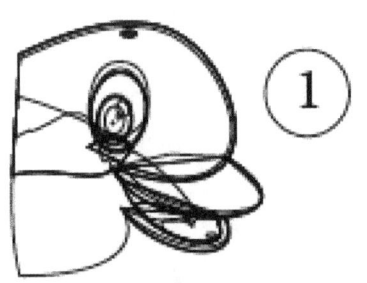
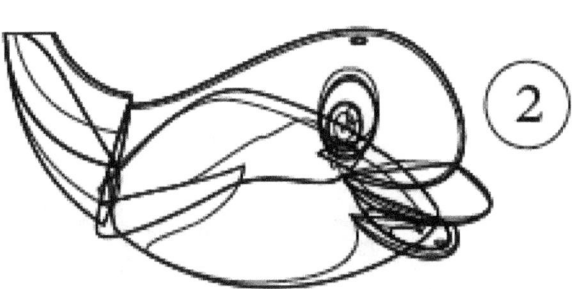

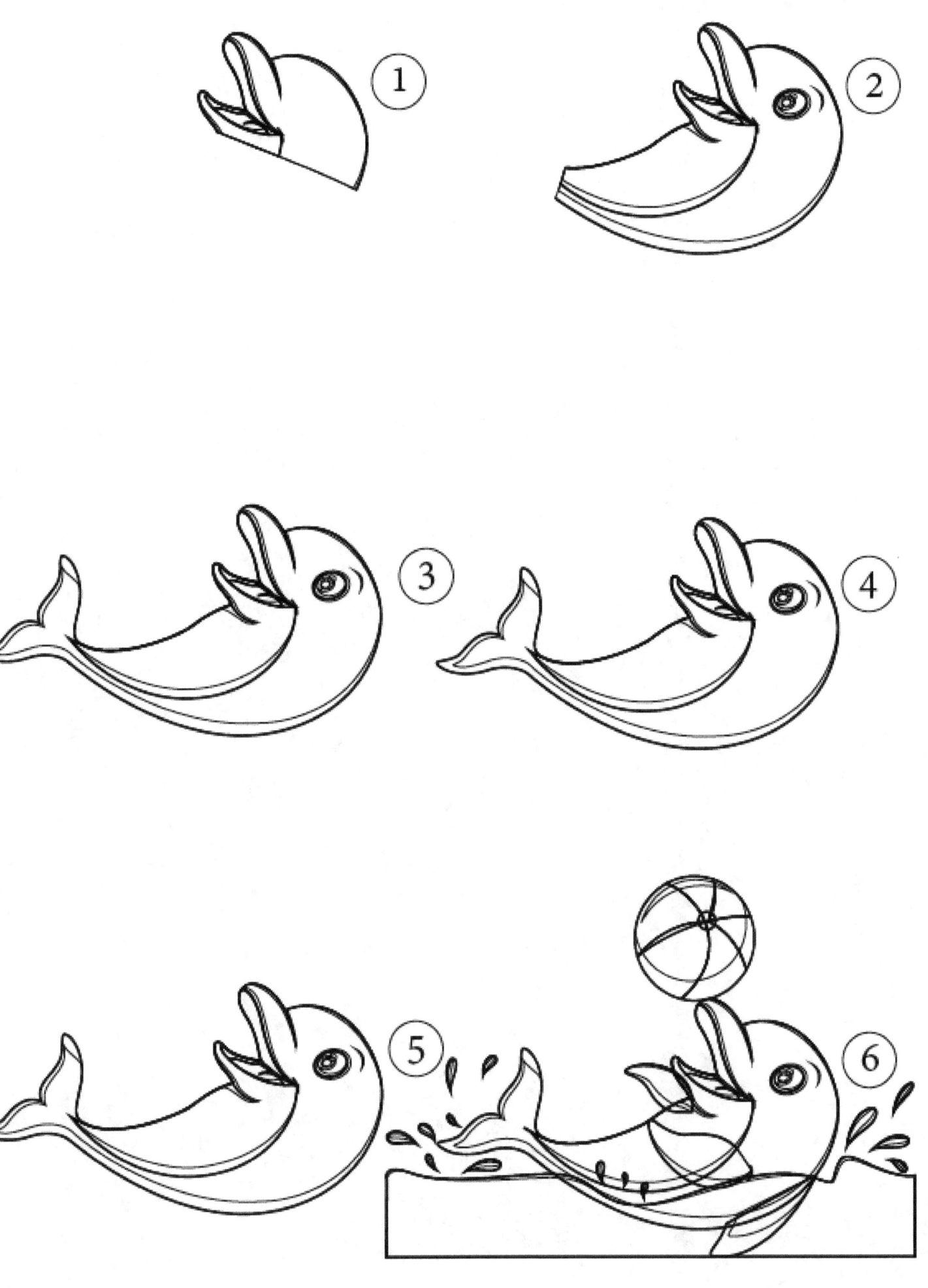

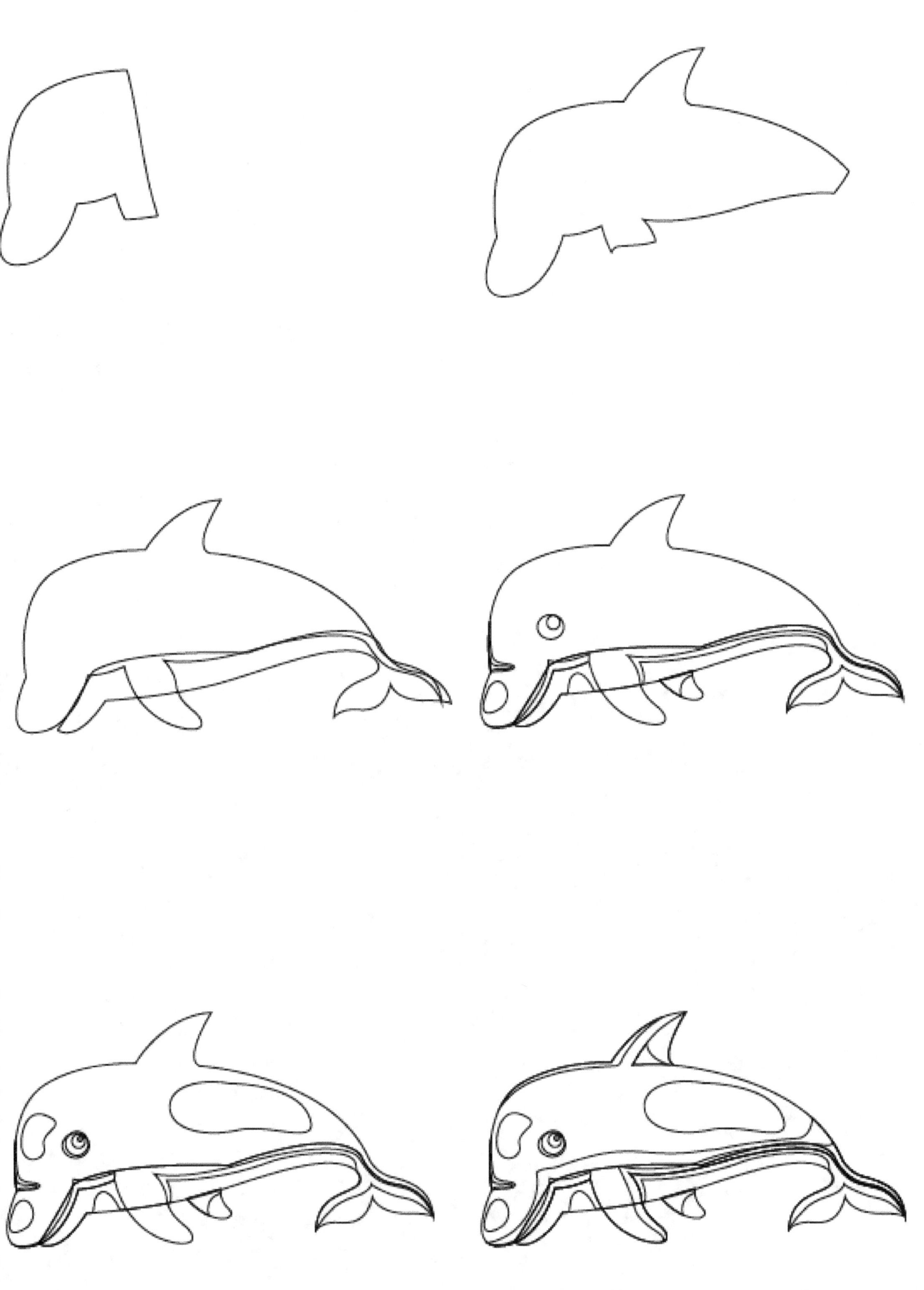

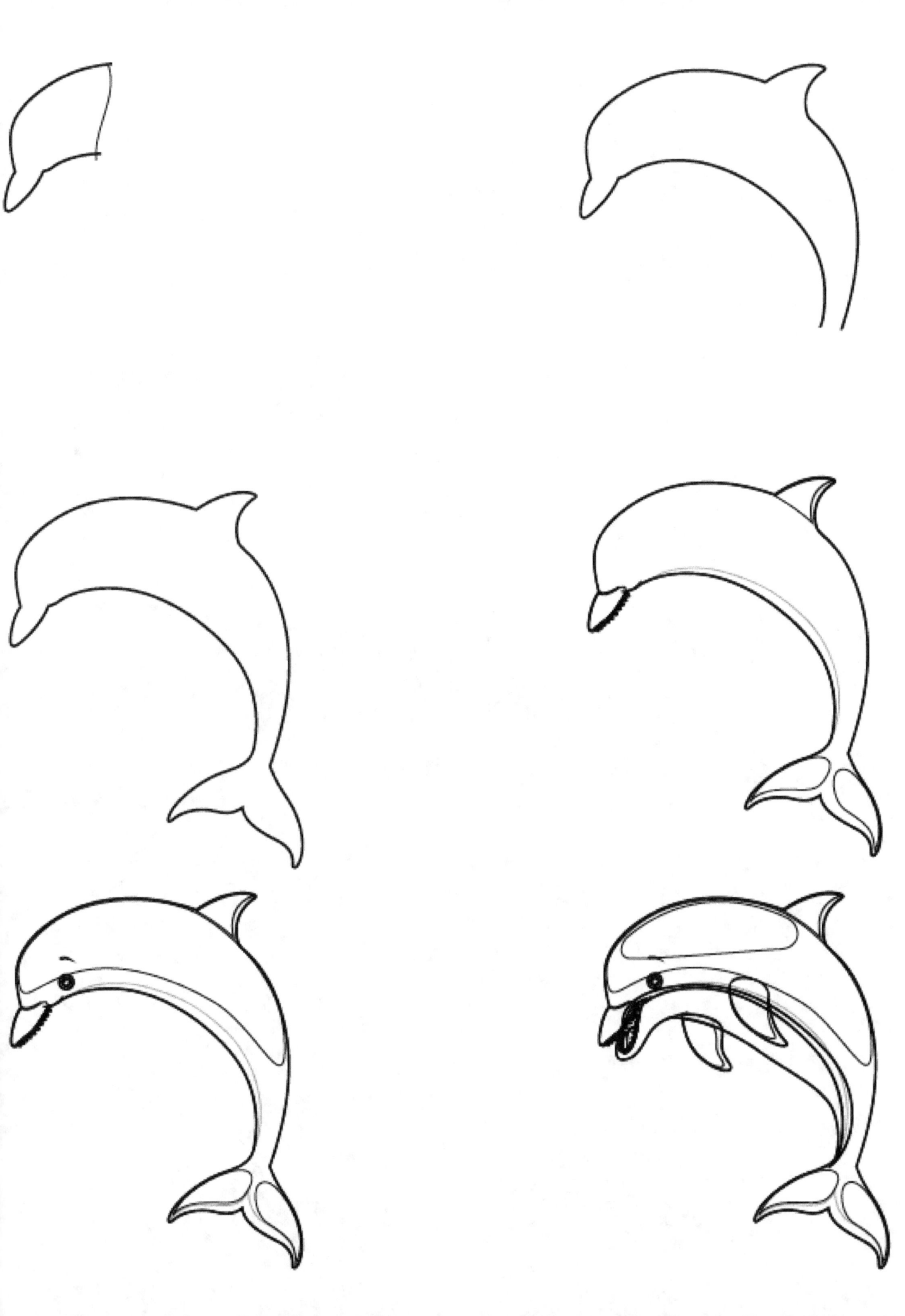

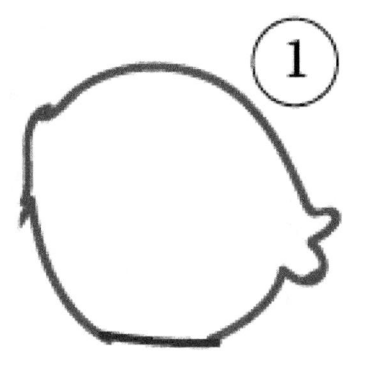
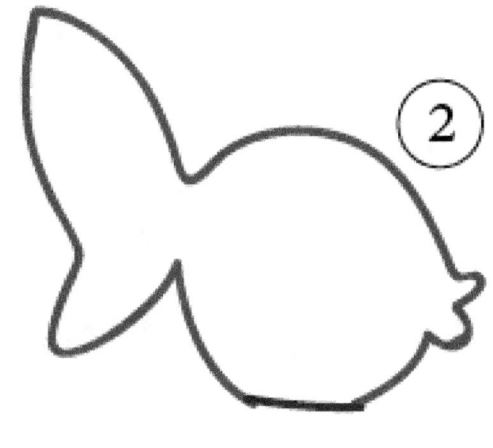

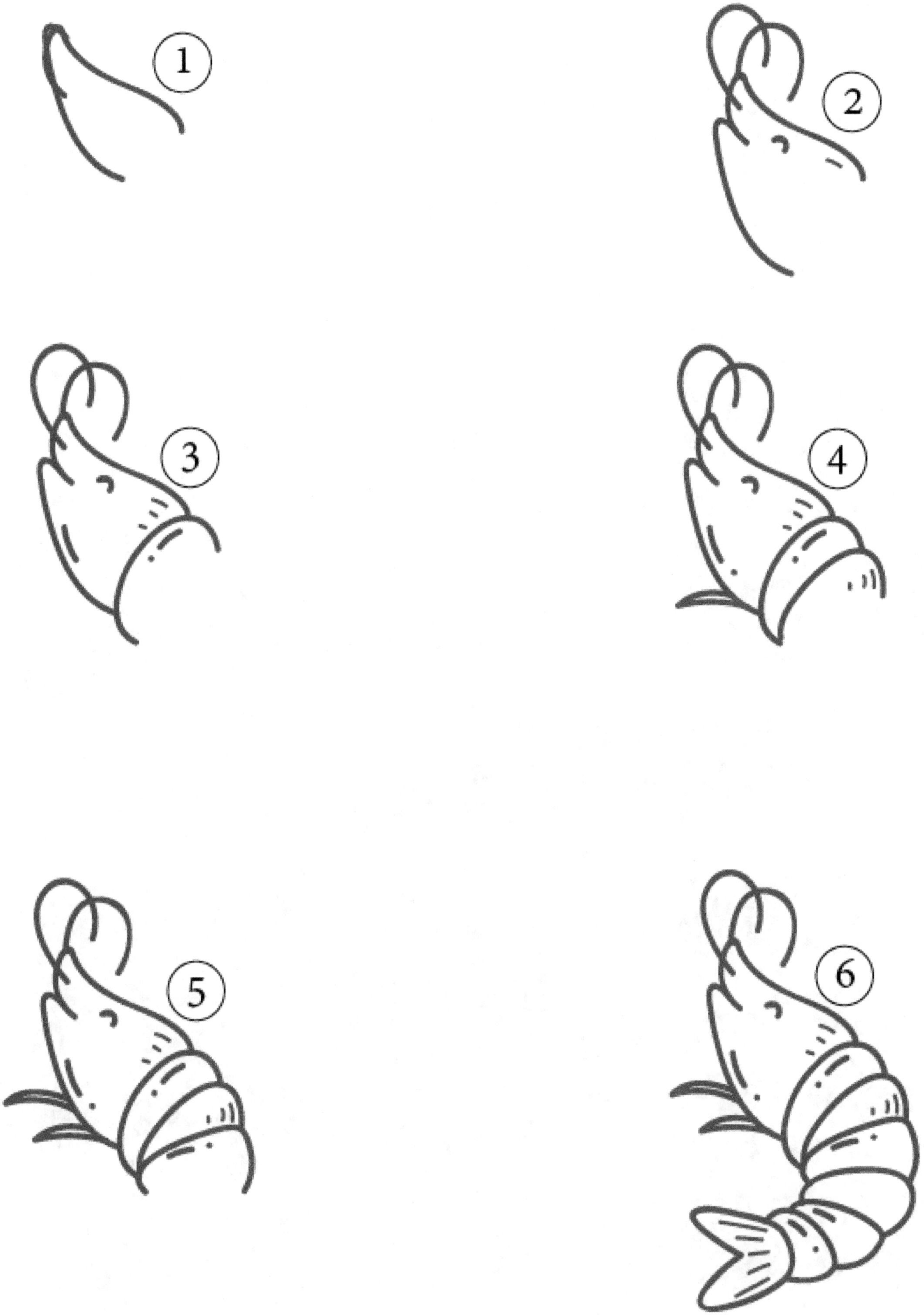

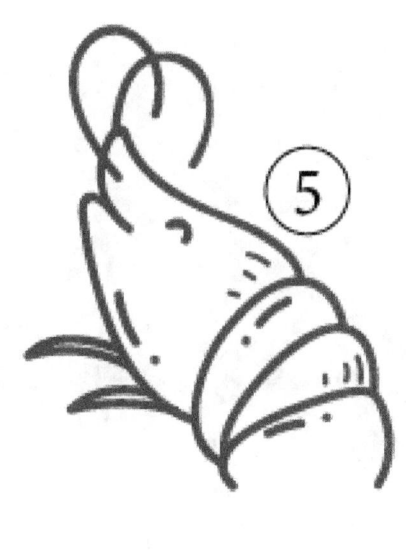

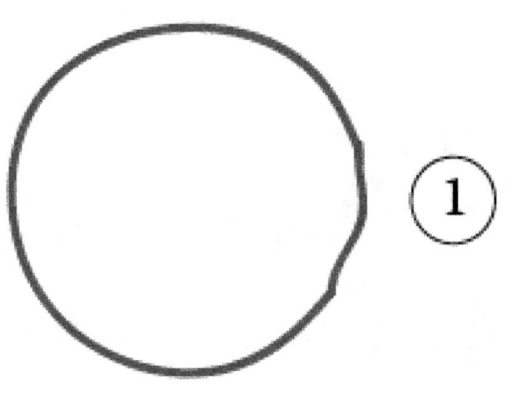
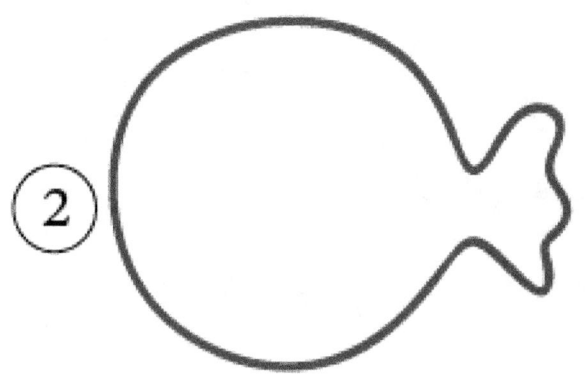
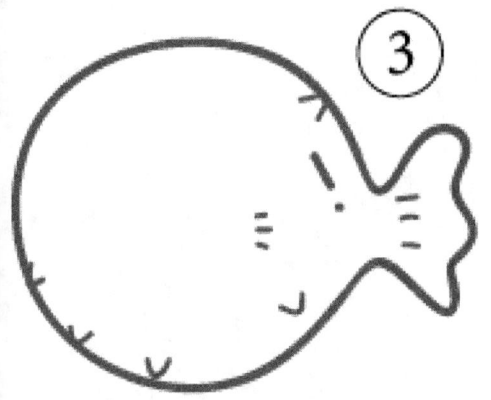

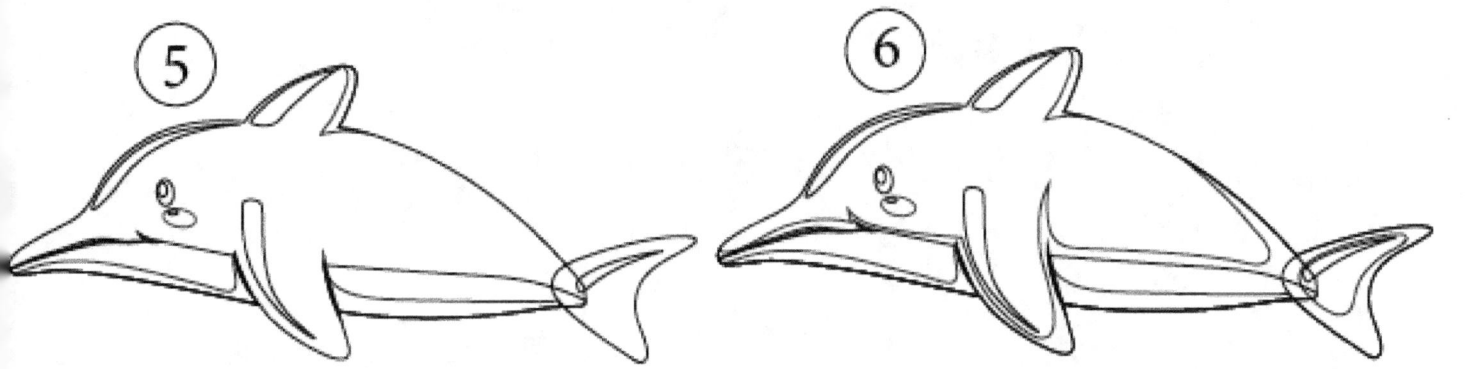

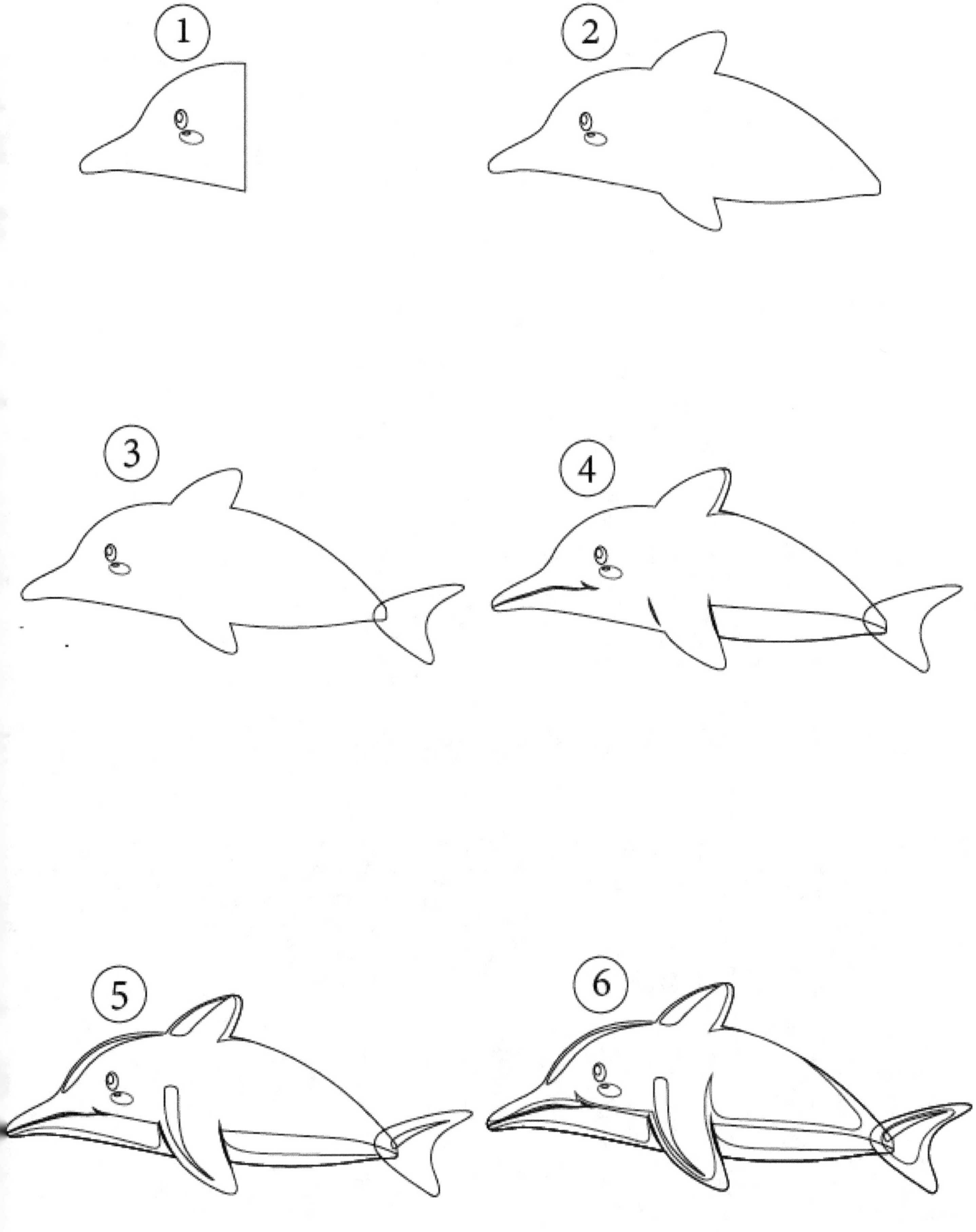

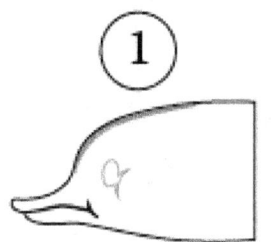

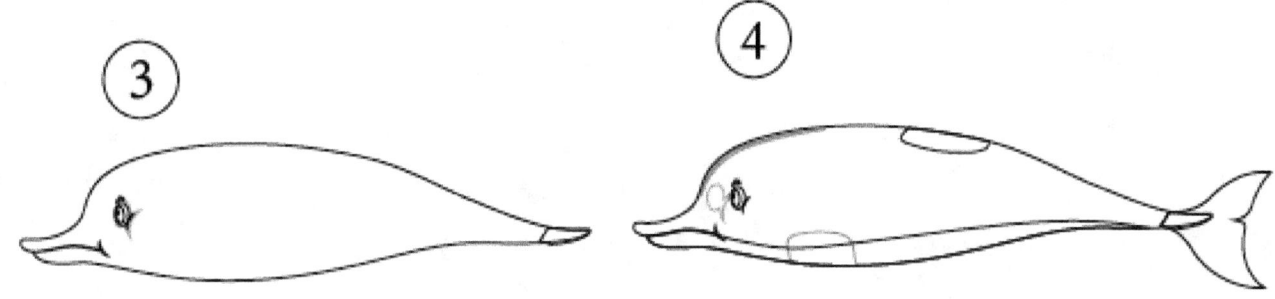
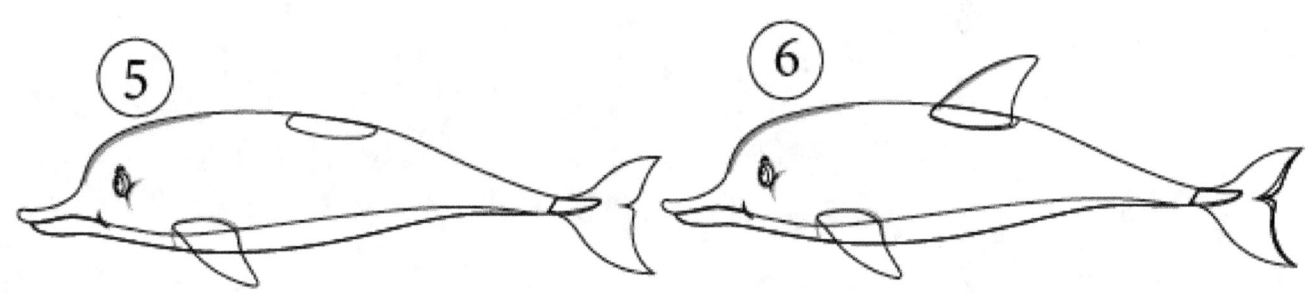

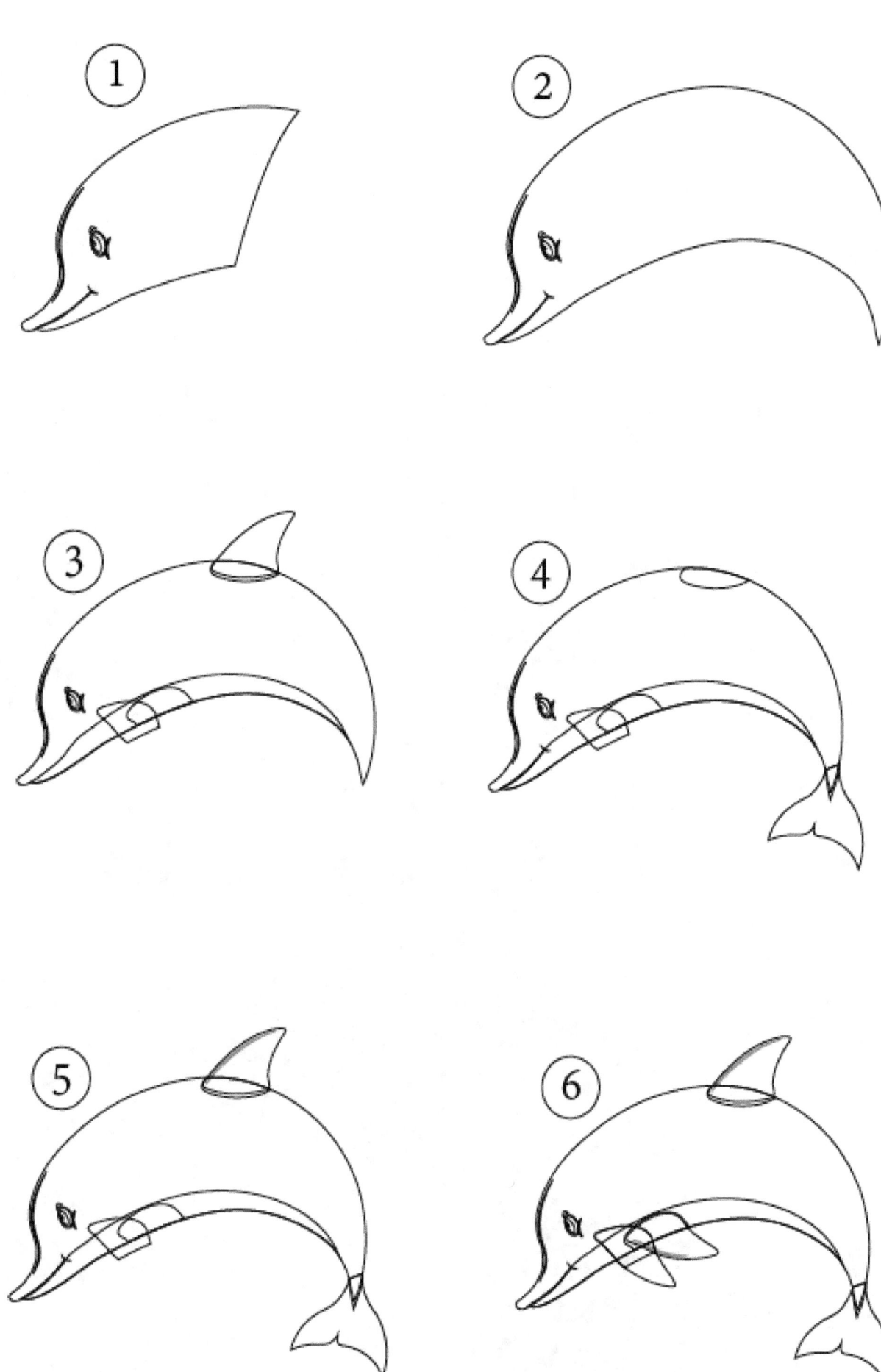

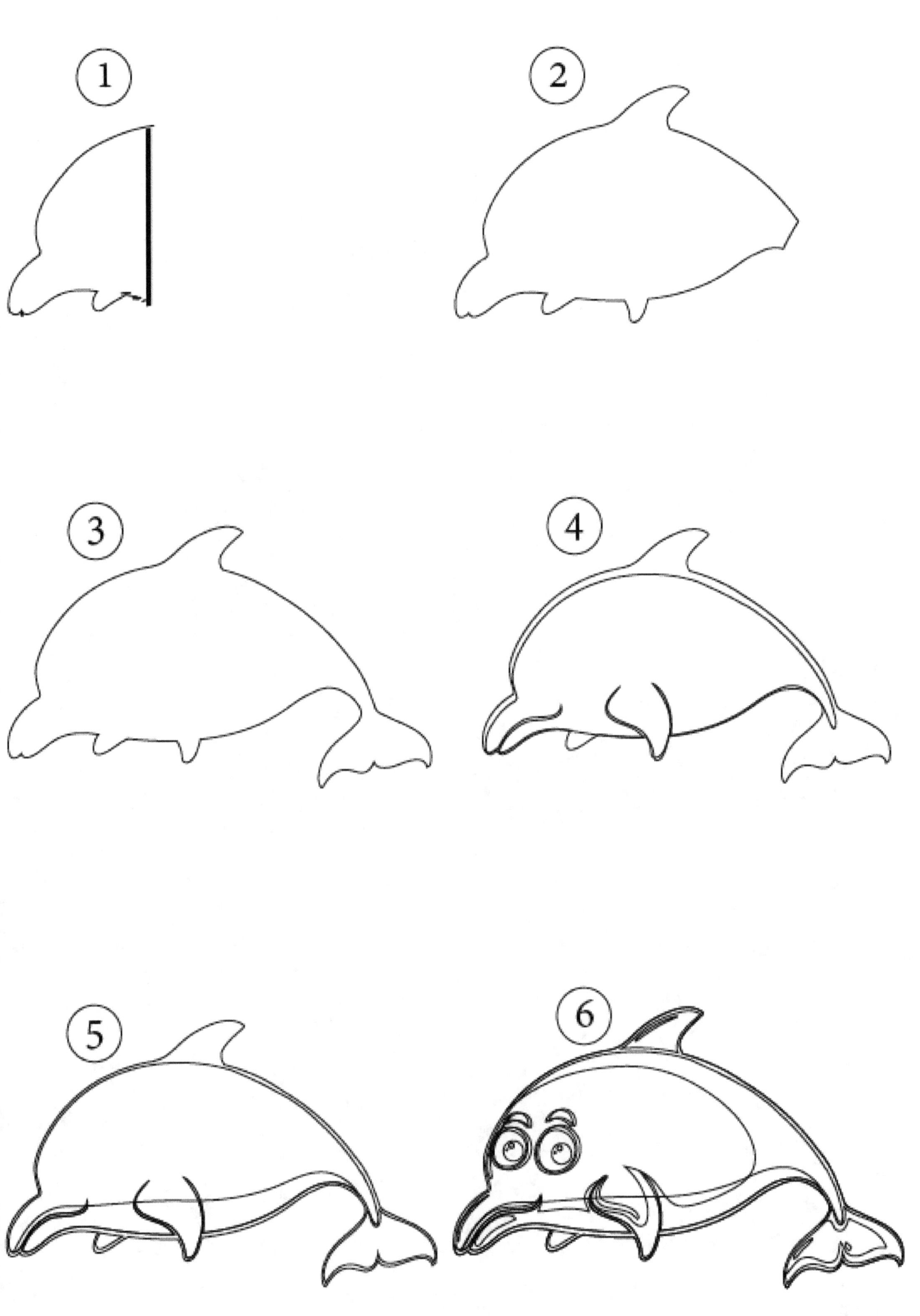

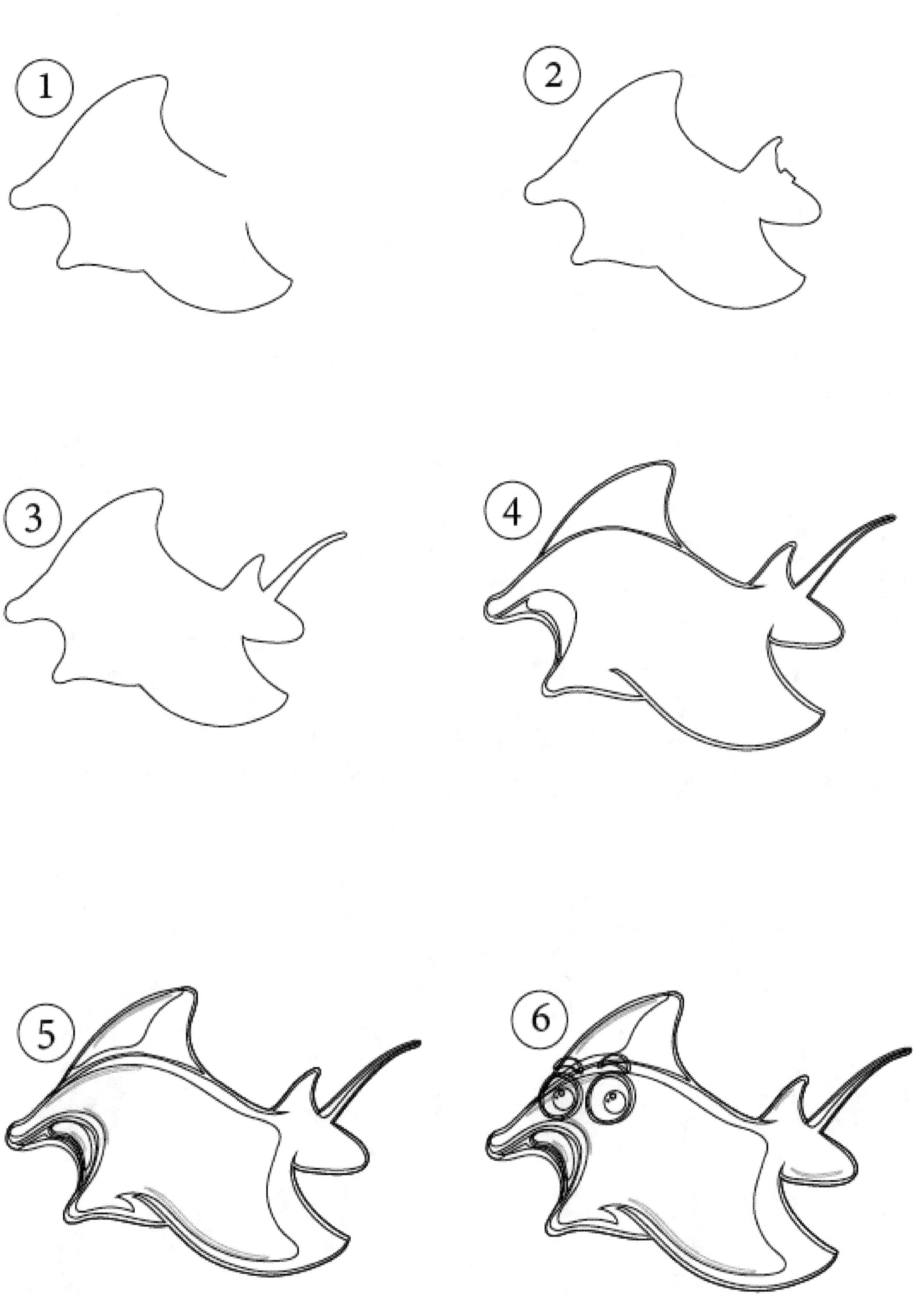

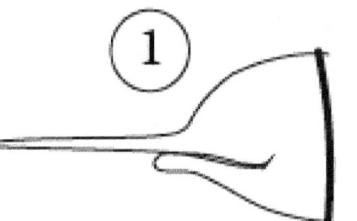

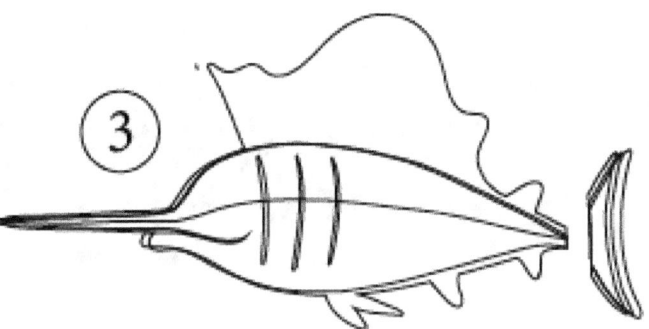
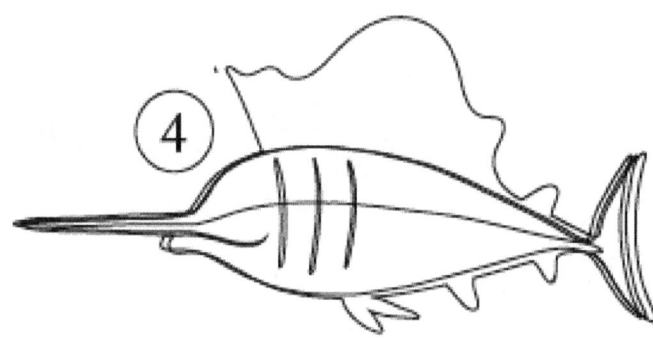

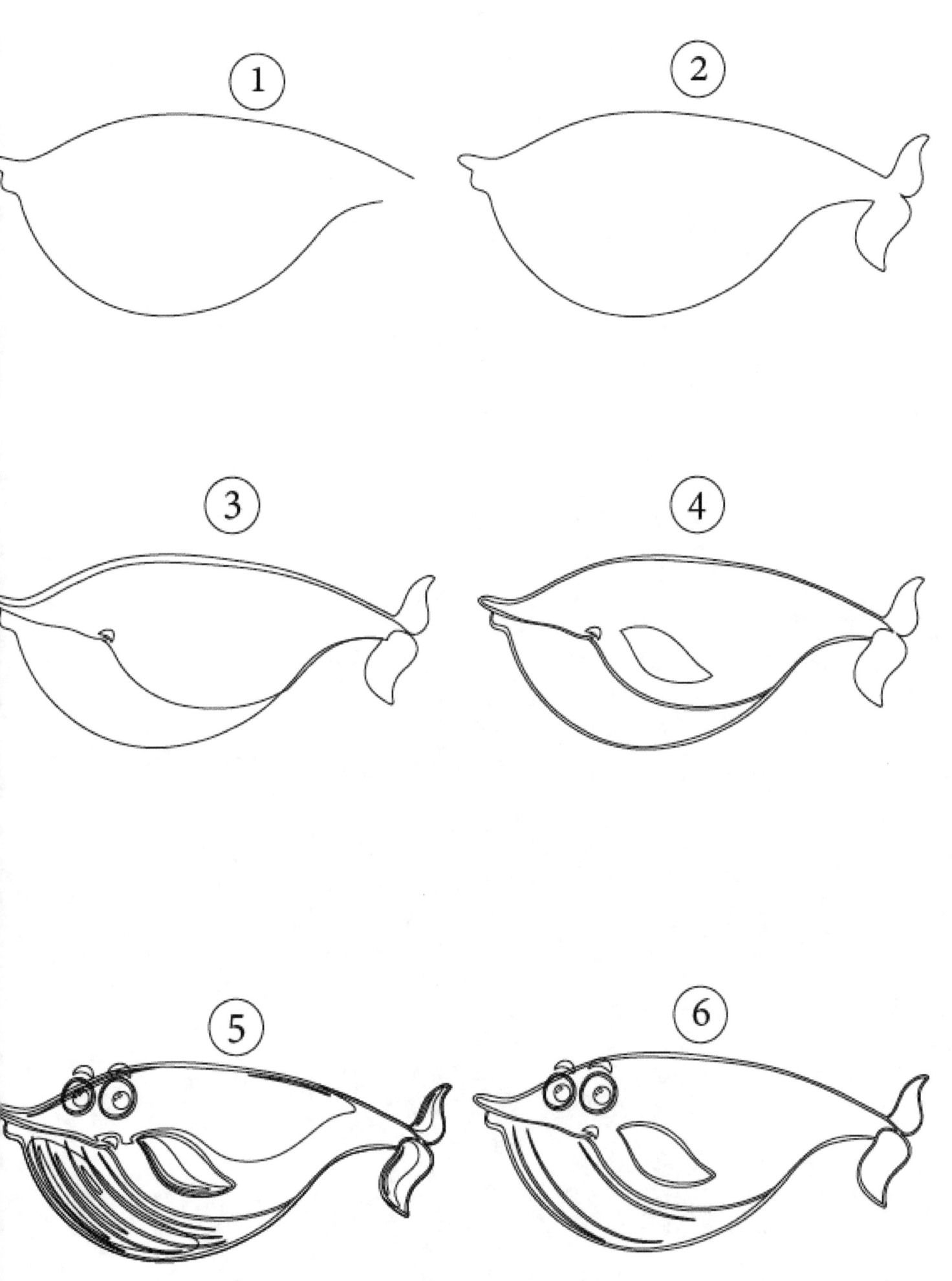

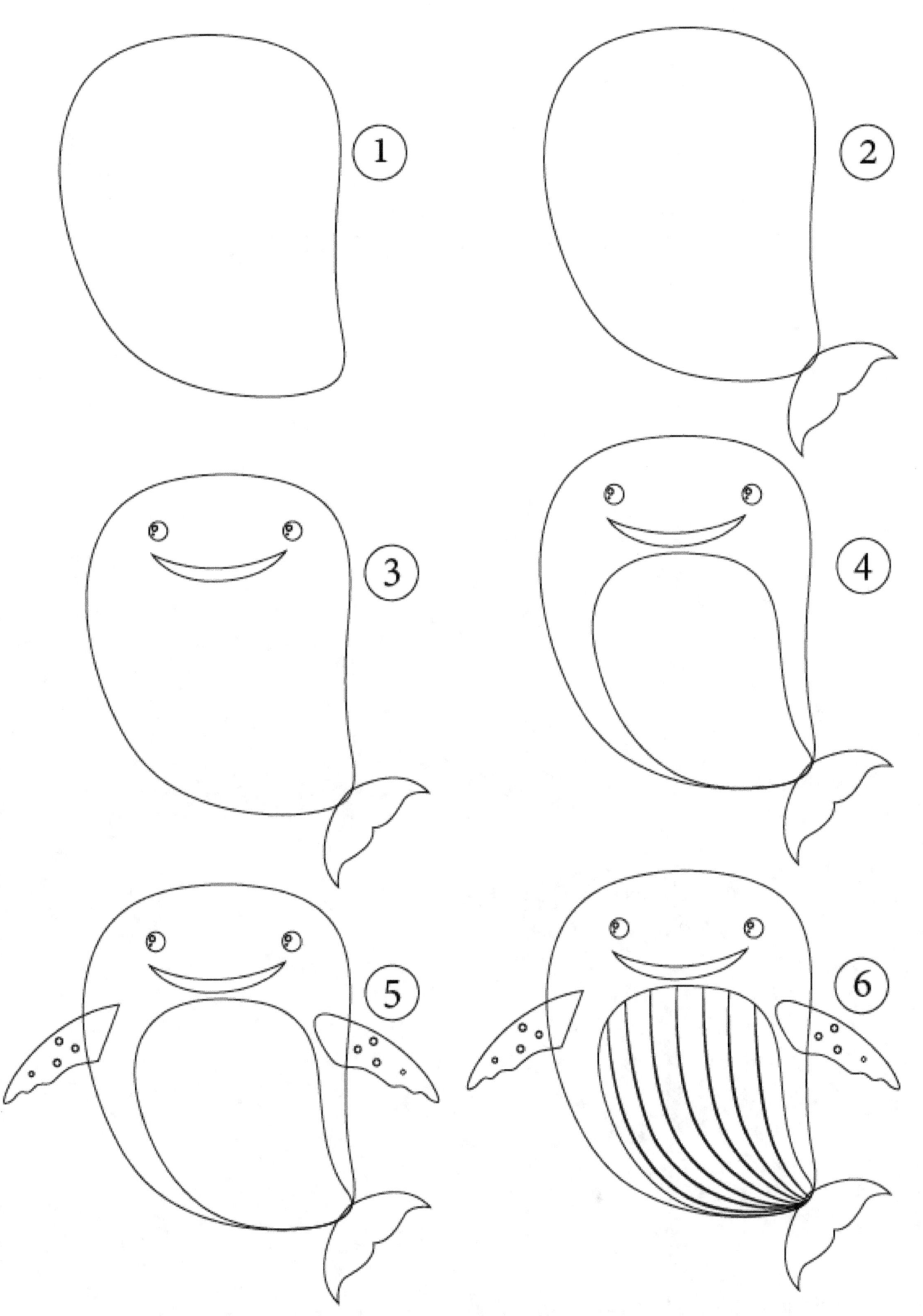

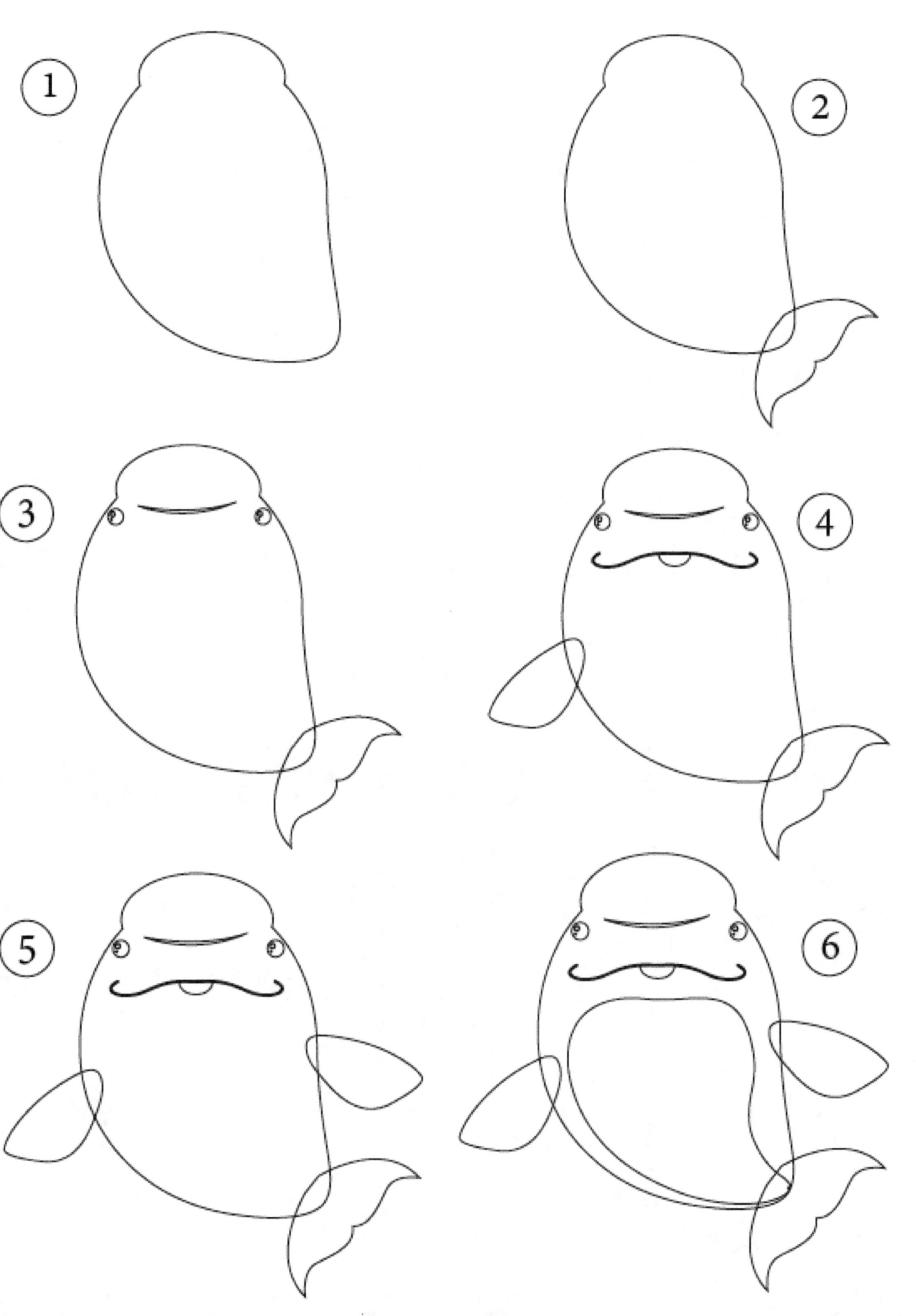

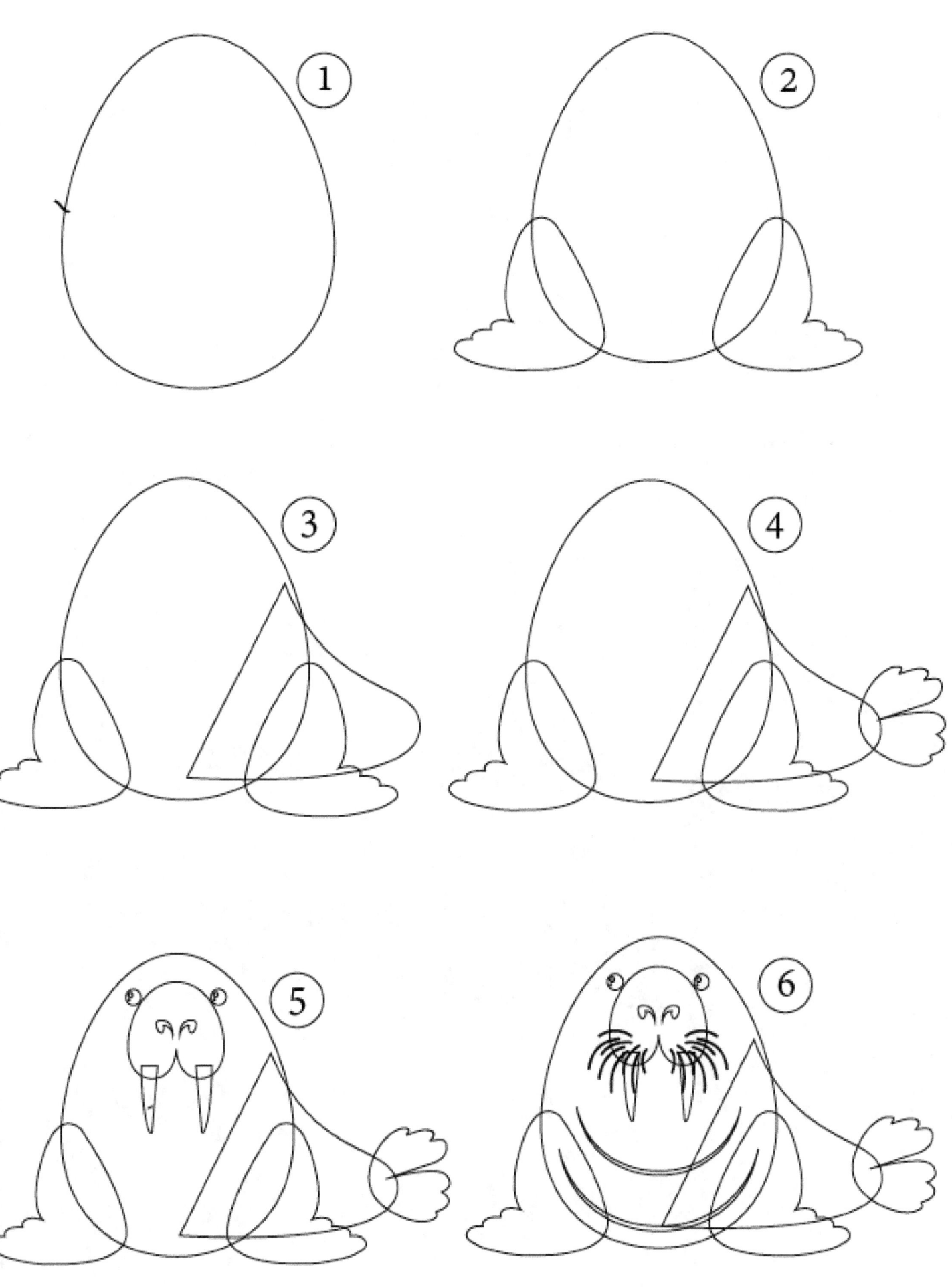

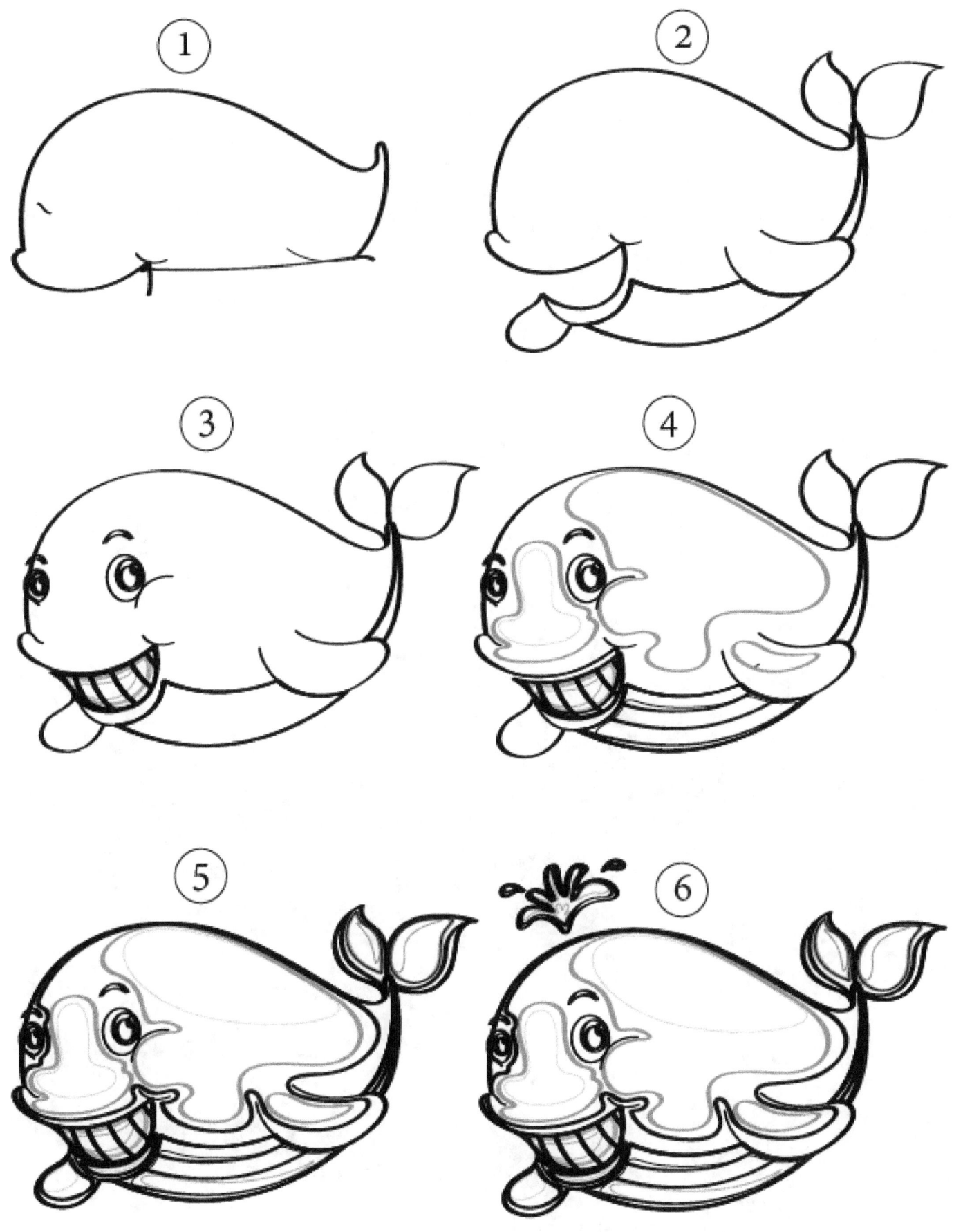

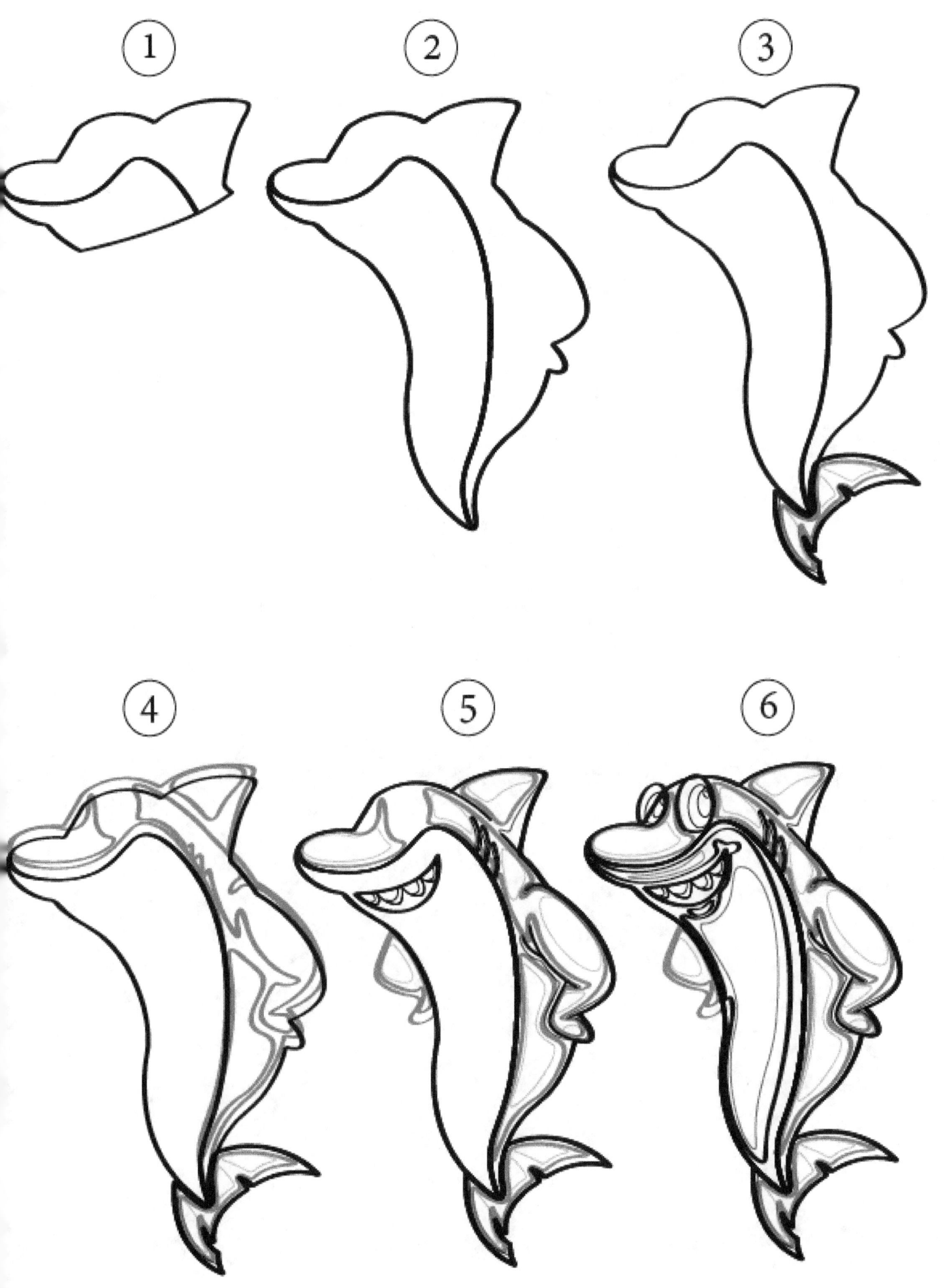

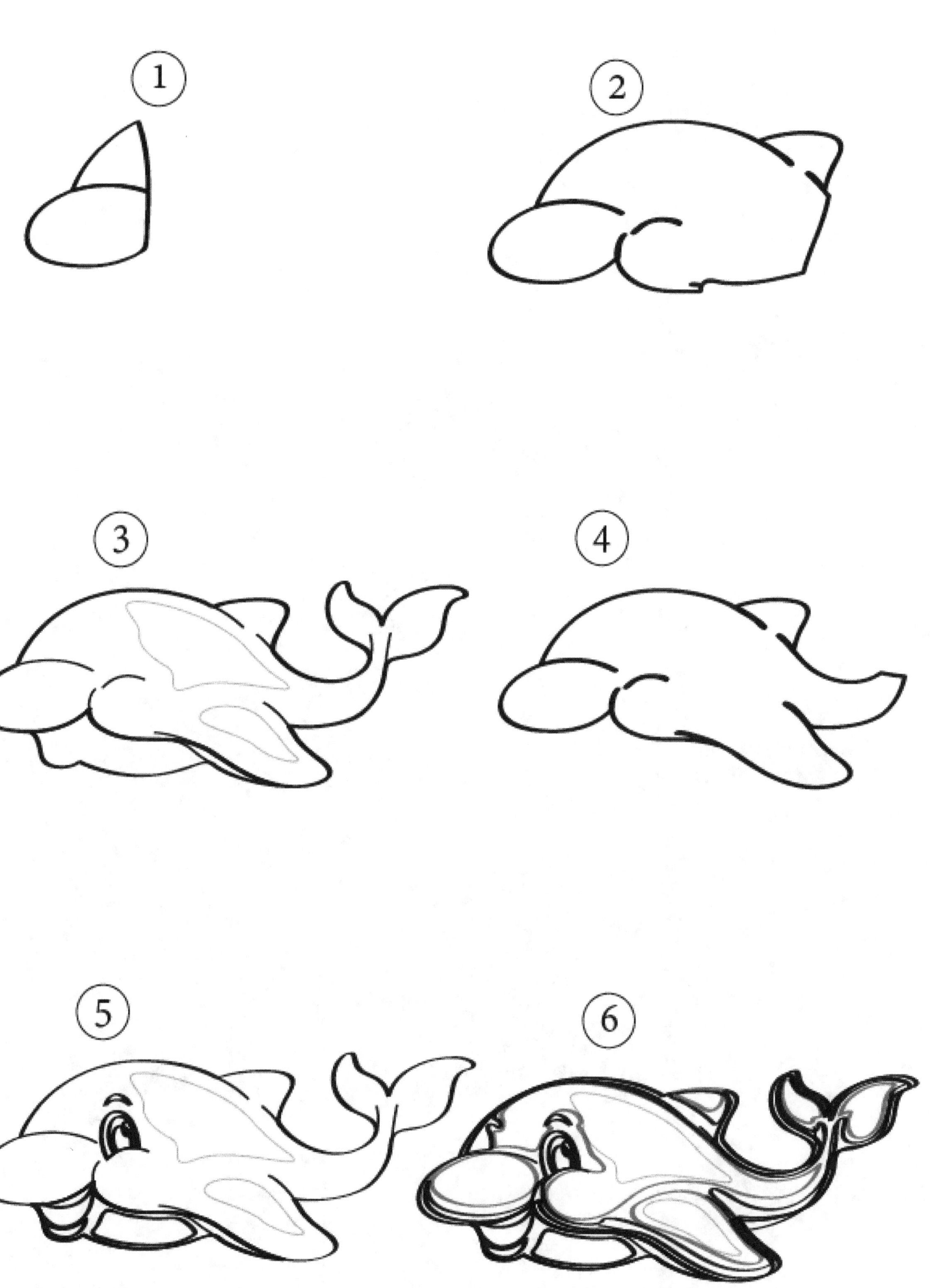

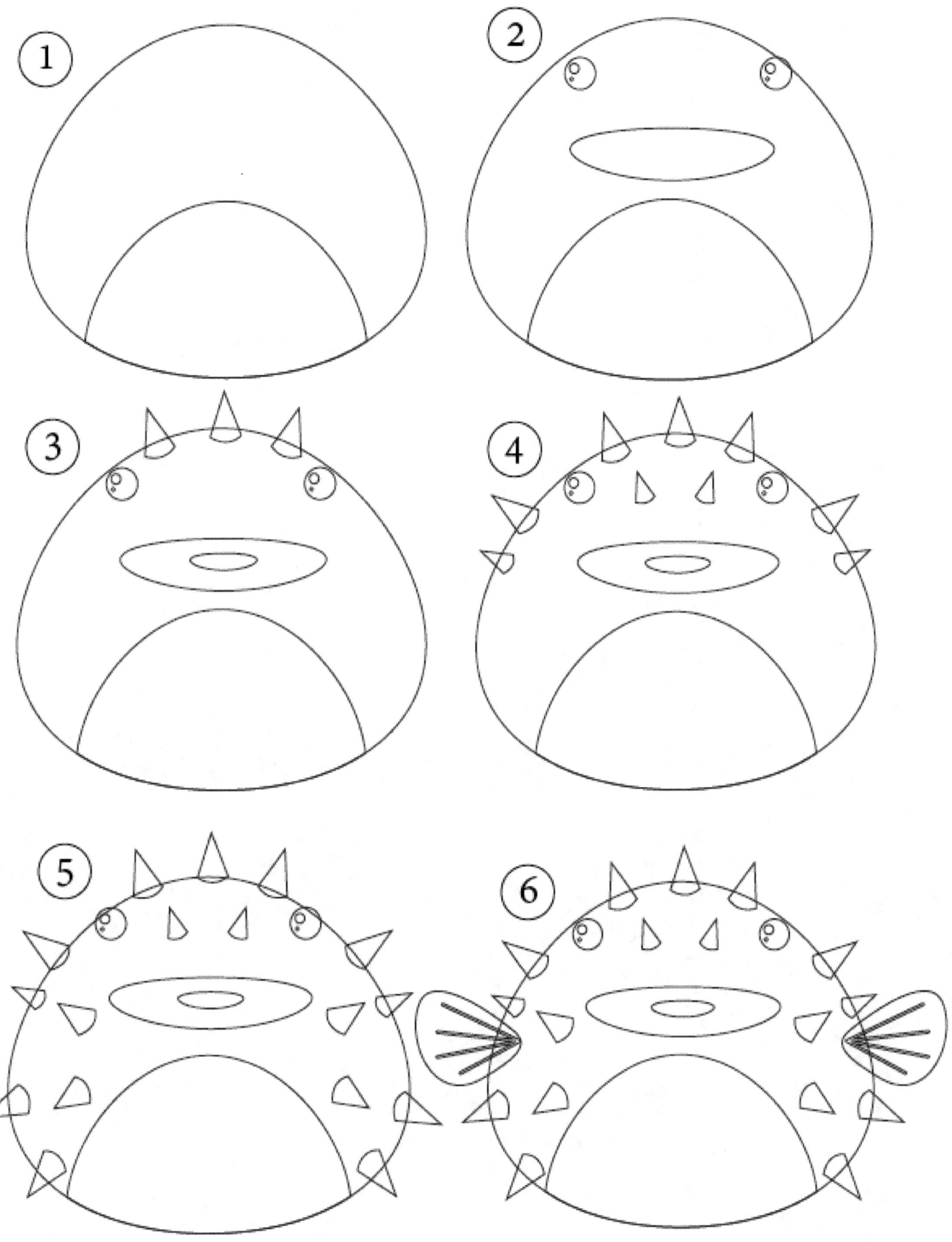

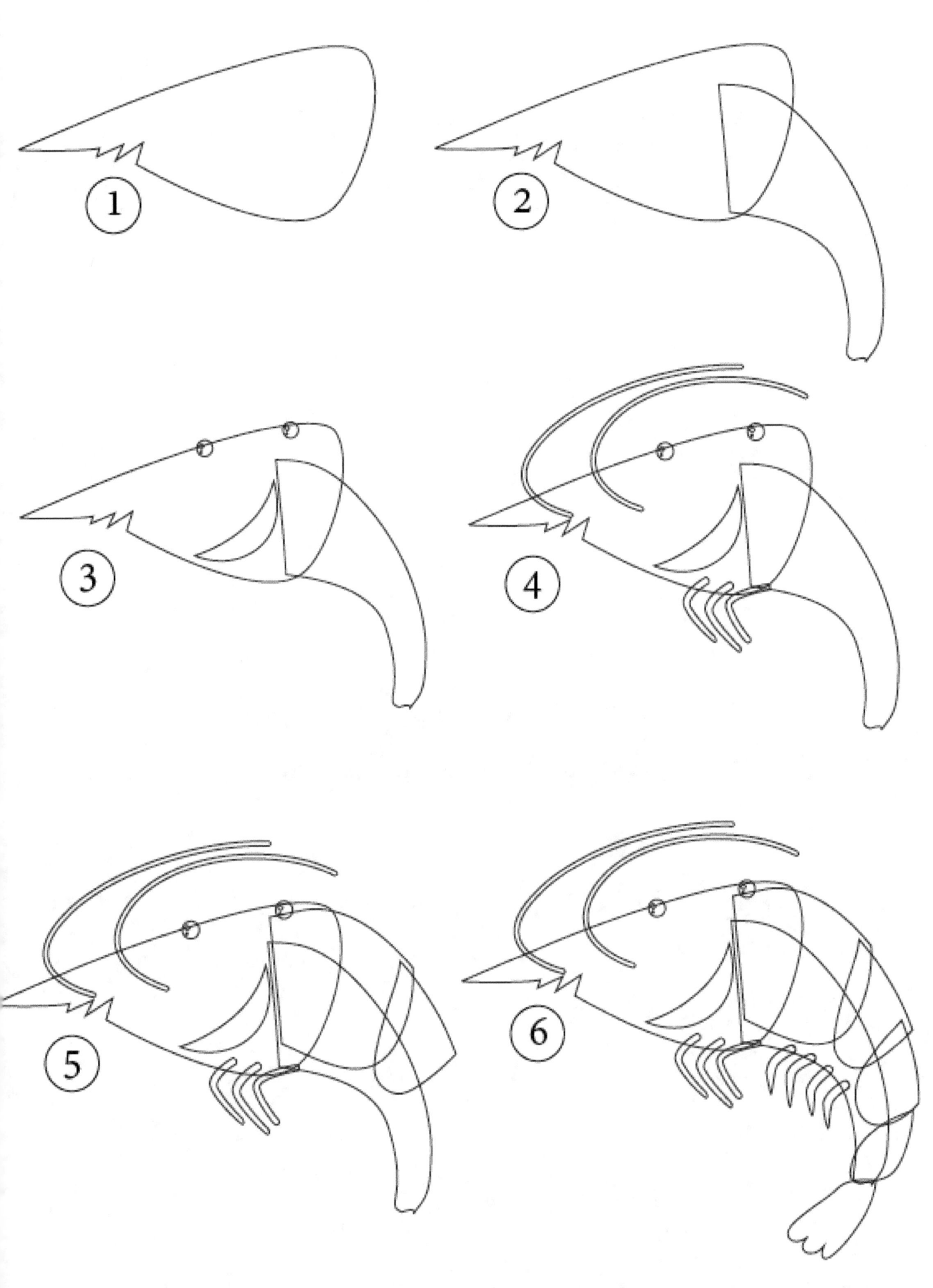

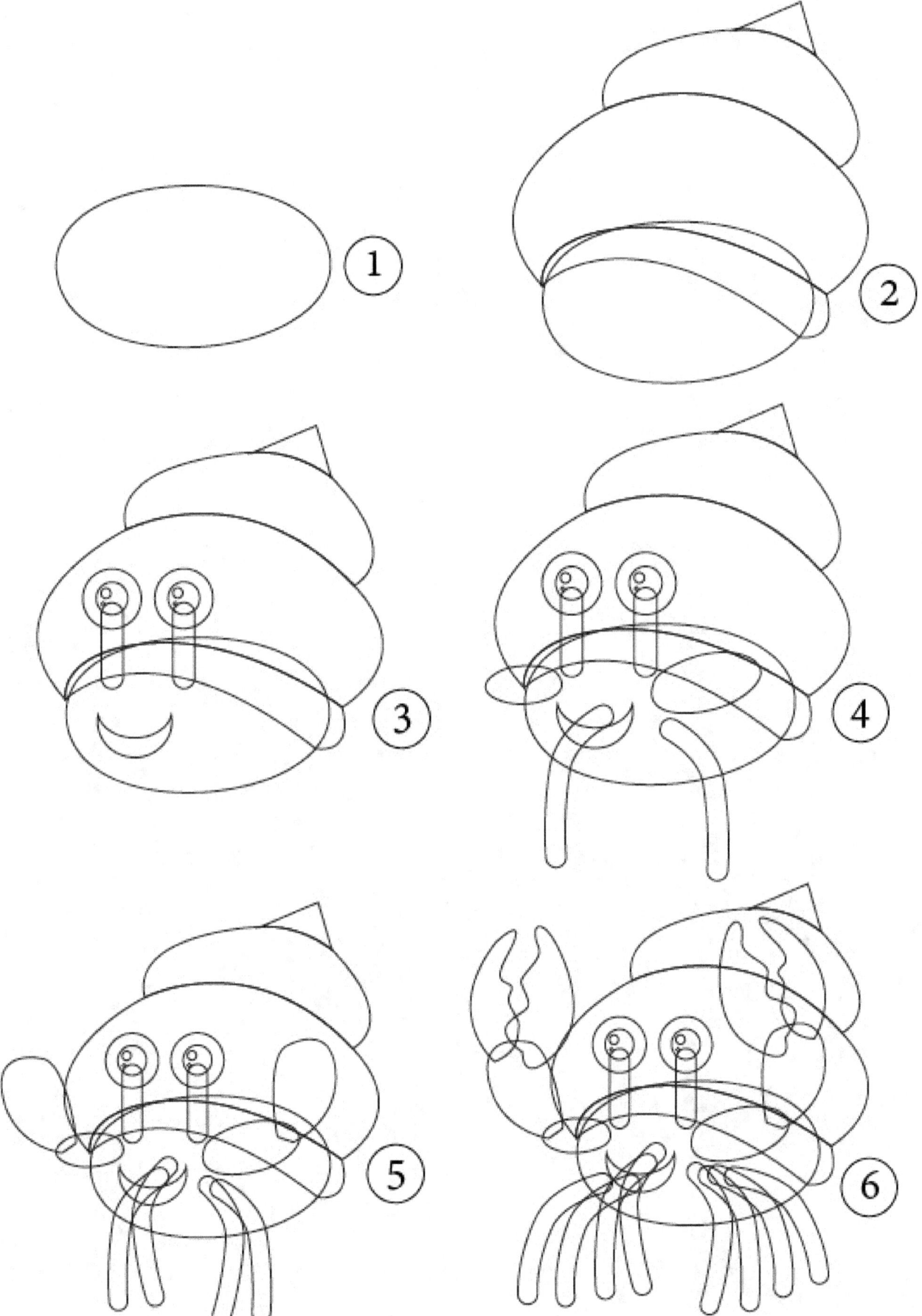

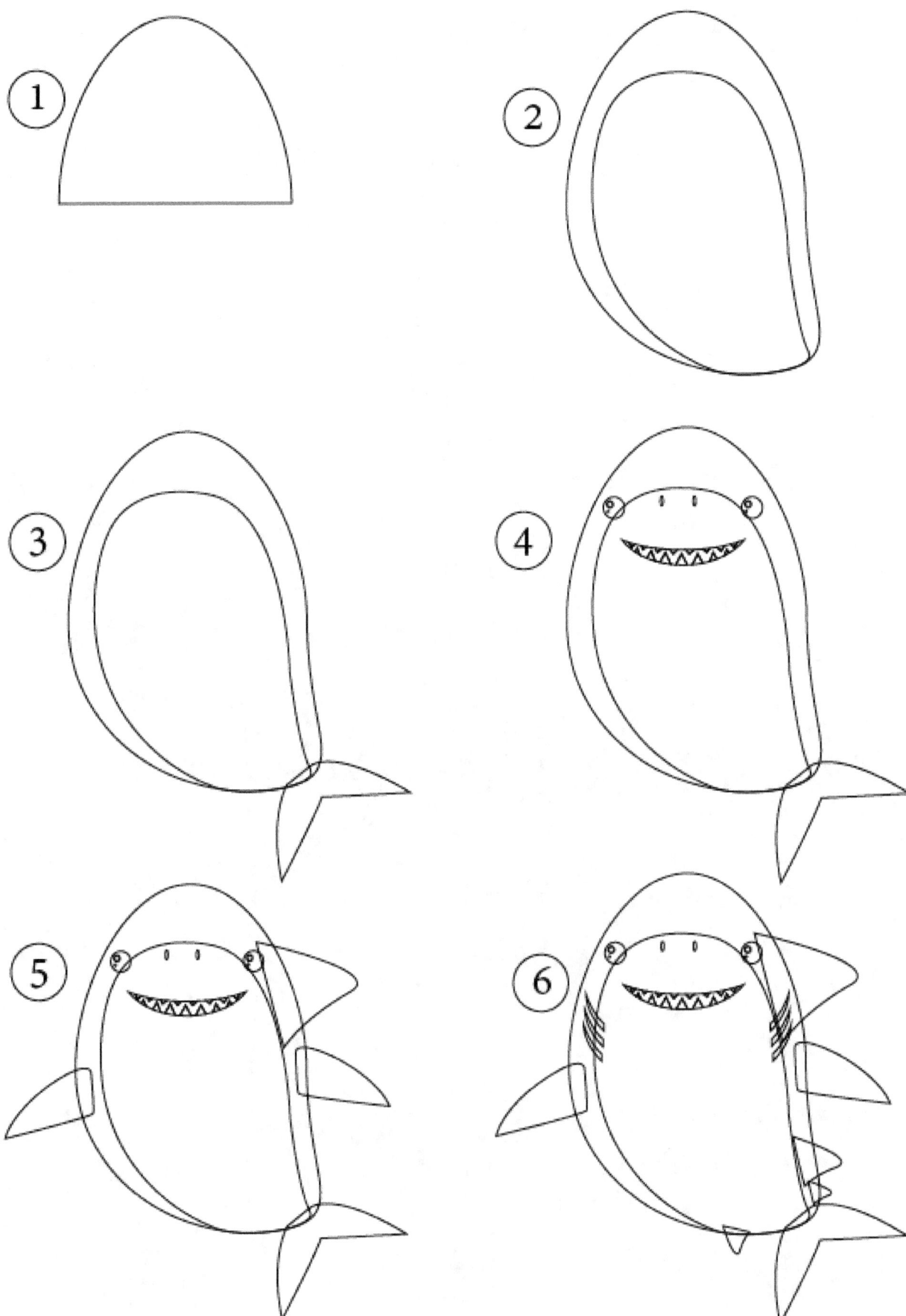

www.ingramcontent.com/pod-product-compliance
Lightning Source LLC
Chambersburg PA
CBHW060430220526
45465CB00008B/3080